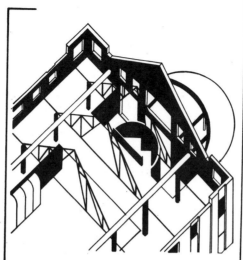

Courthouses
in
Georgia

1825 - 1983

Courthouses in Georgia

Text and Photographs
by
Robert H. Jordan
and
J. Gregg Puster

Editing and Design
by
Patti Anderson
and
Mary Jackson

THE ⬥ HARRISON COMPANY, PUBLISHERS

3110 Crossing Park • P O Box 7500 • Norcross, GA 30091-7500

Dedication

To those valiant men and women of Georgia
who planned, built and paid for their
Courthouses, this book is gratefully dedicated!

Published by The Harrison Company
3110 Crossing Park, Norcross, GA 30071

Photographs and Text Copyright © 1984 by The Harrison Company
First Edition, 1984

Inquiries should be addressed to
The Harrison Company

Printed in the United States

ISBN 0-910694-01-X

Table of Contents

AUTHORS' PREFACE

This is the story of the courthouses in Georgia. The historical events and the persons who played prominent roles serve as a backdrop — or scenery — for the heritage and tradition which is, in reality, the "Biography of Georgia."

The courthouses are the actors and your reaction (as our reader) serves as the action deemed essential in every drama.

Many of the events are familiar; our goal is to present them in the perspective of the courthouse — the view, as it were — from the balcony, clock tower, the lawn or beside the memorial to those who "gave their last full measure of devotion" for an ideal.

The courthouses fascinate many people — Georgians as well as casual visitors and passers-by. Our interest is shared by many. Our collection of hundreds of photographs made over a span of a decade is by no means "exclusive": many a person with even a simple camera has preserved on film his own reaction to the "personality" of the courthouse, just as we have tried to do.

Our research, as comprehensive as it is, is by no means complete; nor is our story of Georgia's courthouses intended to be the ultimate. It may, and should spark more interest in these sometimes over-looked, sometimes taken-for-granted symbols of the sovereignty of the people — our neighbors in our own county.

If we have awakened or aroused your interest in the courthouse in your county, then indeed we feel we have accomplished, to some extent, the goal we set for ourselves quite a few years ago.

> Robert H. Jordan
> J. Gregg Puster

August 15, 1984
Norcross, GA

PUBLISHER'S PREFACE

The research and writing of this publication was completed by Robert H. Jordan and J. Gregg Puster. The Harrison Company has relied solely on The Authors for documentation of the facts, and the related anecdotes.

> The Harrison Company

AUTHORS' ACKNOWLEDGMENTS

The authors express our appreciation to Emily Bradley, James Doyle, Barbara Evans, Beatrice Millican and W. C. Owens of the Sara Hightower Regional Library; and to Kenneth Thomas, Jr., historian, Department of Historic Preservation, for the invaluable aid in our research "Off the highways and byways" of local history beyond the scope of the many county histories available in the State Archives.

Also, to Elizabeth Burt for her photograph of the McIntosh County Courthouse at Darien; to Lael Garnett Puster for her photographs of the Lumpkin County Courthouse at Dahlonega and the Haralson County Courthouse at Buchanan; to James K. Lockhart for his photograph of Government House in Augusta; and to Jim Roof for the careful printing of the photographs appearing in this book.

Also, to the Judges, clerks, administrative officers and assistants, commissioners, historical societies, research assistants, clerks of court and their staffs who were so helpful to us in our travels.

And lastly, we wish to express our thanks to the staff of The Harrison Company, with special recognition to Patti Anderson and Mary Jackson for the editing and design of the material submitted by us.

PUBLISHER'S ACKNOWLEDGMENTS

The publisher wishes to express appreciation to its staff for their contributions to this publication:

To Patty Doss, Todd Watkins, Monica Hosaflook, Jim Marion and Bud Hiller for their assistance on the editing and rewriting; to Donna Helms and Mary Kilgore for the typesetting of the manuscript; and to Julie Capelle for paste-up of camera ready copy.

The Publisher

Map of Georgia

Georgia
1733-1983

INTRODUCTION

The County as The Foundation of Representative Government

The political philosophy of "Federalism," the foundation of American government, provides for supreme authority of a central government with limited powers, and state governments with authority not given the central government, based on a written constitution, which when ratified by the people, establishes the sovereignty of the people.

This philosophy is seen in Georgia where the central authority is the state government and the counties comprise the local geographical units with autonomy similar to that guaranteed the states by the Constitution.

Just as the United States Capitol is the symbol of the Legislative, the White House is that of the Executive, the Supreme Court Building that of the Judicial, so is the county courthouse the symbol of the fundamental sovereignty of the people.

One of the first acts of Georgia's Provincial Congress in 1776 established eight counties which were the consolidation of existing parishes of the Church of England. Prior to the Declaration of Independence in Georgia, these parishes had become the political and social hubs of the community, and the church as much a civic center as a house of worship. Long before the ratification of the Federal Constitution, Georgia provided for the separation of church and state with the disestablishment of the Church of England. The clerical authority of the parish became the secular authority of the county.

Within the two-and-a-half centuries since the founding of Georgia in 1733, there have been numerous constitutions, written and amended as needed to meet changing conditions within the state, many of these directly concerned with meeting those changes in individual counties.

It is of more than passing interest that the "Rules and Regulations of 1776," often considered the first Constitution, which created the counties, required each to provide a courthouse and jail at the expense of the local residents. Each was authorized to elect local officials and to levy and collect taxes necessary for the function of the county government.

Of equal, if not more importance, the county was the territorial division to provide elected representatives to the General Assembly, a principle which recognized the sovereignty of the people as far back as the Magna Carta.

With the ever-increasing complexities and perplexities of modern society, political as well as economic, the importance of the county as the foundation of the philosophy of federalism and the sovereignty of the people cannot and should not be minimized.

# # # #

GEORGIA, THE LAP-BABY OF THE COLONIES

The political structure of Georgia under the Trusteeship — 1733-1751

The first settlers to the new Colony of Georgia were still living in tents after their arrival 12 February, 1733, when General James Oglethorpe established the first rules which, during the Trusteeship, eventually became the law of the land providing the authority to conduct public affairs and business.

The Colony was governed from London and Savannah, with the Charter giving the Trustees complete power, providing that all local laws were approved by the King.

In July, the settlers met at Johnson Square to name the streets for the town Oglethorpe had designed. Each block consisted of ten lots, with four blocks per tithing, or ward. At the center of each ward was a public square with lots set aside for churches, schools, stores, and other nonresidential buildings. For more than a century — until 1850 — Savannah had only six wards.

The Trustees created the "Town Court of Savannah and Precincts Thereof" with three justices, called bailiffs, and a recorder. The Trustees appointed constables and tithingmen who were to summon juries and execute warrants. The constables acted as prosecuting attorneys and served as officers in the militia. The tithingmen were officers in the guard, which had been created before the first settlers had sailed from England.

In 1735, the same "local government" was set up for Frederica, but the outlying areas had nothing. All officials served at the pleasure of the Trustees. Those included the storekeeper, school masters, clergymen, collectors of the port, naval officers, and other port officials. As the Colony grew there was need for a recorder, botanist, surveyor, register of land grants, secretary of Indian affairs, receivers of fees from the Indian trade, an agent for the Cherokees, an agent to distribute presents to the Indians, collectors of beneficiaries for the orphans' home, overseers for Trustee servants, prohibition agent, overseer for silk culture, gardener, overseer for public gardens and the like.

Overlapping and lack of defined responsibilities resulted in nothing short of chaos, in addition to a dearth of qualified and educated persons to fill the posts. Oglethorpe, who preferred verbal orders to written instructions, made the most of what was available, with the approval of the Trustees.

The power of the bailiffs developed by evolution as the duties were never defined. The "Rules of the Year 1735" were regulations concerning the settlement allowances, land granting and inheritance questions. There was no discussion or move made to set up any political structure. There was practically no settler participation, other than selecting delegates who were more than likely "suggested" by the governor.

The rules prohibiting rum and slaves drew strong objections, as well as the limitations placed on land grants of 500 acres requiring tail-male — only males could inherit the land. A petition signed by 199 settlers was rejected and the signers considered "malcontents."

The full impact of the rejection was felt a year later with protests ending credit at the Trustee Store, plus the lack of local participation in the governing of the Colony.

In 1741, the Trustees offered a plan which set up courts, one in Savannah, the other at Frederica, which was the initial step in the creation of a "county." Each had a "president" and four assistants with whatever power the Trustees decided to give them. When Oglethorpe failed to name officials for Frederica, it was added to Savannah. Thus the Colony had its first unified government which lasted throughout the Trusteeship.

In an election in 1751, each town or village with ten families was entitled to one deputy. Sixteen deputies from eleven districts elected Francis Harris, a merchant, as speaker. Before the Assembly could meet, the Trustees surrendered their Charter and Georgia became a Royal Colony.

Georgia, Royal Colony — 1754-1775

At the termination of the Trusteeship, Georgia, with a population of about 3,000 extending from a trading post near Augusta to an abandoned fort on St. Simons Island, was an economic shambles.

The Trustees' plan to develop silkworm culture and establish grape arbors to produce wine had been a complete failure. Few of the early settlers had any experience as farmers and gardeners. South Carolina had to supply the skilled labor to build the first houses.

Most of the original settlers were dead. Many of the surviving members of their families had moved from Savannah.

The colonists sponsored by the Trustees after 1745 were mainly indentured servants. Those who could pay their way and purchase land comprised the bulk of the incoming settlers and were not subject to the stringent rules and regulations of the Trustees. These were the new Georgians who developed their land holdings, and were responsible for the growing use of slave labor.

There was no political organization in which these new residents could participate or contribute (other than taxes) to the governmental affairs of the rapidly growing Colony.

What social life there was centered around the small villages which sprang up beyond Savannah. The few local laws were concerned primarily with land grants and an elaborate slave code.

The tax structure was based on land and slave holdings which placed the burden on the "free" settlers and not the "wards" of the Trustees. What craftsmen and skilled workers immigrated to the Colony were beyond the jurisdiction of the Trustees, adding to the burden of supporting a "welfare state" through grants from Parliament and gifts from a decreasing number of philanthropists in England.

John Reynolds, the first Royal Governor, was a naval officer who conducted his duties as he might have run a taut ship. When the Trustees surrendered their Charter, all organization ceased to exist in Georgia. In view of the precarious condition of the Colony, Reynolds set up a militia to utilize the competent males of the population in the only manner in which he was familiar and experienced. He issued paper money, since there was no treasury, and particularly because there was no currency available or in circulation. He set up a General Assembly consisting of a Council of twelve men appointed by the Crown, and two ex officio members. The Common Assembly provided for nineteen members to be elected by the colonists.

The war between England and France was spreading. Georgia was defenseless, with forts sorely needing repairs; no alliance had been made with South Carolina for any military aid.

With settlers moving north and west, and the traders from both Georgia and South Carolina moving more and more into Indian territory, relations with the natives left much to be desired.

There was the constant threat of the Spanish in Florida and the French in Alabama.

With conditions worsening and Reynolds unable to cope with the complexities of administration, he was recalled to England where he was permitted to resign as Governor of Georgia. He rejoined the fleet, and as an admiral waged war against the French.

Henry Ellis, appointed to succeed Reynolds, was an Irishman, wealthy by inheritance, an explorer, scientist, and geographer with no training or experience in government. Aware of the pitfalls that beset Reynolds, Ellis moved cautiously to gain local support. Each able-bodied male was required to serve so many days each year in public works. Ellis pulled them off road building and set them to work erecting a palisade around Savannah and strengthening the fortifications of the area.

In 1758 the Church of England was established as the official church of the Colony dividing it into eight parishes. This was the first step to set up any kind of local autonomy. The wardens and vestrymen of each parish were empowered to assess and collect taxes for the support of the church, and were responsible for the maintenance of the property and "relief of the poor."

Since there had been little organized religion in the early days of the Colony, membership in the Church of England was not required for election to the vestry. Gradually, the parishes assumed more secular responsibilities and the churches became the center of civic and social activity, as the Colony worked itself out of the paternalism and protection of the Trustees.

Ellis built a fort above Augusta and his appeal to London for military aid was answered with 500 muskets and 100 soldiers. Restless by nature, Ellis soon became bored with the duties and responsibilities of Governor and asked to be relieved. His request brought prompt action; his resignation was quickly accepted.

James Wright, whose family had been active in government in South Carolina, was named the third Royal Governor in 1760. He had formal legal training in England and was well versed in the English provincial system of colonial government.

With the end of the French and Indian War, Wright was able to expand the Colony to the south, now free of the Spaniards, and to the west where the French had lost their hold in Alabama.

The Creek Indians, deeply in debt to the traders, ceded lands of more than a million-and-a-half acres between the Ogeechee and Savannah rivers, and another half-million acres between the Ogeechee and Altamaha rivers. The sale of the land paid off the debts and Wright was delighted when settlers flocked in from the Carolinas and Virginia.

This expansion helped establish a firm economic foundation in the Colony. Trade with the Indians and the West Indies, as well as England, began to flourish.

Social and civic activities centered around the church, with each parish generating an increasing interest in community needs, and the political aspects of the colony and its relations with South Carolina and the other settlements to the north and east.

With a cornerstone of law and order, the Assembly gradually assumed more responsibilities. Participation and interest in local affairs increased to the point that Wright frequently adjourned the Assembly when he couldn't control controversies without the help of London.

With the enactment of the Stamp Act in 1765, Wright sold a few to sixty vessels in Savannah harbor — one of the few such instances in all the Colonies — and drew the wrath of the Georgians. When Parliament repealed the Act, Wright believed the government had reacted to mob pressure.

He rejected the choice of Noble Jones, whose family was among the original settlers, as speaker of the Commons House. When Archibald Bulloch, noted for his anti-British stand, was chosen in place of Jones, Wright adjourned the House.

When the news of the Boston Tea Party arrived in Savannah and the resulting "Intolerable Acts" placed Massachusetts virtually under martial law, protest meetings sprang up all over the Colony.

Prior to his sailing for England to be knighted by George III, Wright appointed James Habersham as acting Governor. In 1773, when Sir James Wright returned to assume his duties as Governor, all was quiet.

By then the seeds of local self-government, planted around the parish church, had taken root. The last semblance of the passivity of Trusteeship days was gone. With the support of the people, as expressed in public protest, the leaders of the anti-British faction were able to establish the Provisional Congress.

Meeting in Savannah in 1775, the Congress took over the local government, ignoring Wright who quickly realized he could not uphold the authority of the Crown. Aware that Georgia was disintegrating as a Royal Colony and that his power as Governor had vanished, he left for England in February of 1776, five months before Georgia's delegates to the Second Continental Congress signed the Declaration of Independence.

Within two months of Wright's departure, Georgia had created a new government with a Provincial Congress issuing a temporary constitution, the Rules and Regulations of 1776. Archibald Bulloch was elected President of the Provincial Congress in July 4 of that year, and became Georgia's first republican governor.

The Provincial Congress during the War Years — Georgia's Constitutions of 1777, 1789 and 1798

The Rules and Regulations of 1776, also known as the Constitution of 1777, were written by the members of the Provincial Congress and adopted without popular vote. Each county had ten delegates to the Assembly, except Liberty, largest by population, which had fourteen. The Constitution was brief, based somewhat on the principles of the colonial government, with emphasis on representation at the local level, the county, and with due regard to English Common Law.

Each of the eight counties, formed from parishes of the Anglican Church, were named by the Assembly and authorized to build a courthouse and a jail, at local expense; to elect delegates to the Assembly, a clerk of the court, a sheriff, a coroner, and constable, each to serve for one year. The probate judge and the justice of the peace were appointed annually by the Assembly.

Each county was required to keep all public records, register probates, and establish public schools to be funded by the state. Taxes were based on land holdings and slaves. It was an implied power that each county could assess and collect taxes based on the bills passed by the Assembly.

The judges of the Superior Court, appointed by the Assembly, were to meet twice each year in each county to hear criminal cases, those involving land grants and probates. Each county had a court of conscience, presided over by the justice of the peace in civil cases, where not more than ten pounds was involved.

When the Declaration of Independence was signed, Georgia had a population of around 50,000, including slaves, spread along the coast and extending into the upcountry which comprised much of the Creek Cession of 1763. Economic growth was paced by the large rice and indigo plantations bordering the marsh regions, with the small upland farmers providing foodstuffs, small grains and cattle. Most of the trade, prior to the outbreak of the Revolutionary War, had been with England and the West Indies. The merchants and shippers, serving as factors, were also the bankers filling the void of little currency, no banking facilities and limited credit.

Georgia's provisional government assumed power and responsibility, without any credit, with a currency not readily acceptable outside the state, no financial stability and no means for defense against the British and their Indian allies, the Creeks.

Of the initial issue of currency by the Continental Congress, Georgia received none, since there was no Georgia delegation to that meeting. Another serious problem was the efforts of South Carolina to annex Georgia.

When the British took over the southern coastal area occupying Savannah, the Assembly met in Augusta with an ever-decreasing area of political influence and control. The county governments were left to their own resources as the upcountry farmers, frontiersmen and traders assumed local leadership. The delegates to the Continental Congress were concerned with the defensive helplessness of Georgia. Agriculture, rather than mercantilism was the state's future.

# # # #

With the British overrunning most of the state, Georgians were hard pressed to take care of their own needs, much less provide manpower, food and clothing for the militia authorized by the Continental Congress. With the capture of Augusta, the Assembly was scattered and Georgia was without any effective government. There was no way to collect the $500,000 appropriated by the Continental Congress for Georgia's immediate needs.

A Supreme Executive Council was formed, and although illegal and unconstitutional, elected John Wereat as Governor, and an Assembly. For the first time in her history, Georgia had three governors, including Sir James Wright, the royal governor in Savannah.

The two rival factions were united after Augusta was recaptured. John Howley was elected Governor, and Wereat headed for Philadelphia to claim the $500,000.

Following the surrender at Yorktown, British fortunes in the South waned. With the abandonment of Savannah in July, 1782, the war, for all practical purposes, was over in Georgia. The Assembly convened there for the first time in four years to pick up the pieces of a war-torn political and economic state. The county governments, battered and bruised, were still functioning at least to the point of electing representatives to the Assembly.

In addition to writing a tax bill (which they didn't) the Assembly faced a bitter border dispute with South Carolina, with the navigation rights to the Savannah River at stake. There was the continuing threat of the Creeks and Cherokees and the renewal of export trade, shortage of shipping during the war virtually eliminated needed imports; local produce for export became local surpluses. The rice irrigation systems, through neglect and the fortunes of war, deprived Georgia of a vital export income.

The cessation of hostilities brought settlers into Georgia from the Carolinas, Virginia and Pennsylvania seeking cheap land. Grants were available for veterans of the Continental Army in lieu of pensions authorized by the Federal government. Georgia was outgrowing the existing rules and regulations. The need for a new Constitution was apparent and the Assembly took action.

The capital was moved to Augusta in 1782, an indication of the growing influence of the upcountry Georgians and the decrease in the political power of the coastal counties. Pressure on the Indians brought Georgia's southern boundary to the Florida line as the Savannah River was opened to inland upstream trade.

The Assembly called for a constitutional convention with each of the counties represented by three delegates. After three meetings, during which the county delegates were shuffled and changed, a new Constitution was written and ratified by the Assembly and became effective 6 May, 1789.

# # # #

The new Constitution followed the Federal insofar as the three branches were separated and provided for a two-house legislature. Each county was to have one senator elected for a three-year term, and from two to five representatives, depending on population, to be elected annually.

Inferior courts were established for each county with the justices to be appointed by the Assembly. As more duties were assigned these courts, additional authority was granted in executive functions with the power to levy and collect taxes to support the local government.

The Governor to be elected by the Assembly for a two-year term, was given power of veto, to grant reprieves and pardons and issue writs of election to fill vacancies.

The Superior Court was to have two sessions a year in each county. The judges, attorney general and other state officials were to be elected or appointed by the Assembly.

The sovereignty of the county was vested in the local election of the senator and representatives to the Assembly.

An important article of this Constitution called for a constitutional convention to be held in Louisville in 1795 and each county was instructed to elect three delegates to the convention.

In less than two decades Georgia's economic growth, expansion westward and northward, with an increasing influx of immigrants, required a government that could keep pace and a constitution that could be amended to meet these changes.

# # # #

The membership to the 1795 Constitutional Convention included delegates from all twenty counties, with seven of the nine new counties in the Piedmont region. Population had passed 82,000. Aided by the invention of the cotton gin and the introduction of long-staple cotton, the growing agricultural economy increased the political influence of the upland counties. Migration was from the coastal areas as well as the Carolinas and Virginia.

The Convention was in session only two weeks and made few changes other than amendments to move the State Capital to Louisville, set the membership of the General Assembly at fifty-one in the House and establish one Senator for each county. The final action was to call for a Constitutional Convention in May, 1798 at Louisville. Each county was authorized to select three Convention delegates at the election for members of the General Assembly.

# # # #

On May 30, 1798, sixty-eight delegates, representing twenty-four counties, signed the document which was to become known as the Constitution of 1795 which served, with only twenty-three amendments, until Georgia joined the Confederacy in 1861. The new Constitution followed the pattern established by those enacted during the formative years of Georgia's statehood. A bill of rights was incorporated similar to that of the Federal Constitution with the specific prohibition of imprisonment for debt (except for fraud) and banning the importation of slaves after 1808.

The sale of public lands was prohibited prior to the establishment of new counties by Acts of the General Assembly, or the alteration of those in existence.

Representation in the General Assembly House was based on population determined by a census to be taken every seven years. Each county was to have at least one but not more than four Representatives and one Senator.

An Inferior Court was established for each county with jurisdiction in all civil cases except land titles. The Superior Court held sessions twice a year in each county to hear criminal cases, civil cases on land titles and appeals from the courts of conscience. The power of a county ordinary, or register of probates, was invested in the Inferior Court which eventually became the administrative, if not executive branch of county government.

Except for justices of the peace and magistrates of the courts of conscience, judicial appointments were made by the General Assembly. Other county officials including the sheriff and coronor were elected with members of the General Assembly.

Several of the amendments concerned county representation in the Assembly as the population grew and the number of counties increased. With the dawn of the Nineteenth Century, Georgia had a population of 162,686, double that of the 1790 census, and twenty-four counties as compared to thirteen when the first census was taken.

After ceding the western lands to the Federal Government and with her own boundaries established, Georgia was the largest State in the Union.

# # # #

GEORGIA, THE YARD CHILD OF THE ORIGINAL STATES — 1800-1861

The Courthouse Becomes the Symbol of Local Sovereignty — 1825-1861

Within the lifespan of George Washington, who led a successful revolution and was chosen first President of the new Republic, Georgians picked up the pieces of a well-intentioned but poorly conceived and mismanaged philanthropic colonial experiment to build the fourth of the thirteen original United States.

Within the lifespan of Abraham Lincoln, Georgians established a strong state government, with counties the foundation of the sovereignty of the people; led a young and growing nation into an era of agricultural prosperity; furnished four Cabinet members and the Minister who brought about Spain's ceding Florida to the United States, and two Presidential candidates. Abraham Baldwin was elected President pro tem of the U. S. Senate serving from December, 1801 to April, 1802. James M. Wayne, Georgia Congressman from Savannah became the first Georgian to serve on the U. S. Supreme Court appointed in 1834 by President Andrew Jackson.

Georgians were among the troops who battled British armies and helped clear the decks for action when "Old Ironsides," built of Georgia oak, took on the English navy in the War of 1812.

Georgians pushed back the Seminoles and Creeks and then marched off to avenge the Alamo. Georgians fought and died with troops from beyond the Alleghanies in the Mexican War.

By 1825 Georgia counties increased from eight to seventy as the population grew from an estimated fifty thousand at the time of the Battle of Lexington to more than 340,000; by 1860 there were more than a million persons living in Georgia.

Within this span of time, Georgians founded the nation's first state university, made provision for public schools within each county, established an asylum for the mentally ill and built so many roads that a State Highway Board was needed.

Constitutional changes had the people electing the governors and almost all county officials except the judges. Ad valorem had replaced land holding as the basis for taxes and a State Supreme Court was functioning.

While a cable was connecting New York with London, and the *Savannah* proved the Atlantic could be crossed by a steamship, Georgians built the Atlantic & Western and the Georgia Railroads. Steamboats plied the rivers with roads connecting the northern mountains where streams powered saw and grist mills.

The hills were probed for gold and coal; granite and marble were quarried and shipped all over the nation. The many uses for Georgia pine opened another industry, naval stores.

Georgians followed the political philosophy of Thomas Jefferson and were staunch Democrats with exceptions — they rejected John Quincy Adams, the last of the Federalists. Twice Georgia voted Whig, losing with Hugh Lamar White and winning with William Henry Harrison.

Even though Herschel V. Johnson was Stephen Douglas's choice for vice president, Georgians supported John Breckenbridge. Lincoln's name was not on the ballot.

Eleven counties are namesakes of Governors who served during this era: Josiah Tattnall, Jr., Jared Irwin, Peter Early, William Rabun, George M. Troup, John Forsyth, George R. Gilmer, Wilson Lumpkin, William Schley, George W. Towns, and Herschel V. Johnson.

# # # #

GEORGIA — THE RAVISHED HAND-MAIDEN OF THE CONFEDERACY

The Civil War through Reconstruction — 1861 to 1876

With the fall of Atlanta in 1864, Yankee troops had little difficulty in crashing into the backyard of Georgia, uprooting the garden, burning down the smokehouse and, after looting the pantry, setting the house afire. Georgia, the breadbasket of the Confederacy, was prostrate. The soldiers, staving off impending military disaster, were slowly starved into submission.

Sherman presented Lincoln with 25,000 bales of cotton which belonged to Georgians as a "Christmas present" after destroying railroads, bridges, factories, mills, public buildings — including several courthouses — and many private homes.

Once fertile farmlands were scorched, farm tools and implements rendered useless. Seed supplies were fed to the ravens which followed the invaders.

Civil government at the local level ground to a halt as the miliary took over enforcing the decrees of reconstruction at the point of bayonets. Efforts to call the General Assembly into session found few legally qualified legislators as most white Georgians were defranchised — they could vote but they could not hold public office. What eventually met with the approval of the provisional government accomplished little, other than to abolish slavery, repudiate Georgia's war debt of eighteen million dollars and let the 1861 Constitution stand, with repeal of the allegiance to the Confederacy. County ordinaries were authorized to administer the oath of amnesty as the provisional government struggled to establish Georgia under the harsh terms of Reconstruction.

During the war, the counties, through the inferior courts, issued bonds and levied extra taxes to equip volunteers and support the indigent families of the Georgians who were fighting on all fronts. The

University of Georgia was closed and the facilities used for refugees. Other schools and colleges were converted to hospitals where friend as well as foe was treated alike.

Thousands of blacks, now wards of the Freedman's Bureau, roamed the state crowding into cities and larger towns to await Christmastide when the land would be divided into 40-acre farms complete with a mule.

Hoping for economic recovery, additional cotton acreage was planted, only to be dashed with crop failure. Drought in the northern counties doomed the grain crops. Army rations kept Georgians and freedmen from starvation.

The banks were closed. With the suspension of specie, the paper money was worthless. There was no source of capital to repair the railroads, get the factories back into production, or plant crops. Large plantation lands lay fallow as there was no reliable source of labor. The need for mechanical skills was left unfilled as returning young veterans were attracted to the cities and towns, preferring to be clerks rather than farmers or factory hands.

The county governments were encouraged to resume regular business and the courts authorized to administer the oath of amnesty. In 1871 the General Assembly, meeting the requirements of the military government, endorsed bonds for expansion of the railroads sorely needed to move northern commodities and manufactured goods into the South.

Aware that Georgians were pulling themselves up by the straps of their tattered boots, these bonds were financed without a heavy tax burden on the people. The economy at the local level received a boost as the smaller towns and less densely populated areas had railroad service.

Most of the carpetbaggers were gone by 1872 when the Democrats regained complete control of the state and with that, the return of the Great Seal. The Department of Agriculture was established and with realization of the natural resources of Georgia, the office of State Geologist was created.

During this period, courthouses, paid for with Confederate currency, were completed in Banks and Brooks counties.

Small farms were replacing the large plantations resulting in the increase and growth of small towns so in 1870 the Legislature created Douglas, McDuffie, Rockdale, Dodge counties and in 1875 Oconee County.

With the end of Reconstruction, Georgia began the second hundred years of the United States with a population of 1,184,000, an increase of only 27,000 since the 1860 census, and 135 counties. Fifty-five thousand Georgians gave their "last full measure of devotion" for ideals and principles.

"If the revolution of civil war and reconstruction wrought anything of an enduring value, (wrote Clara Mildred Thompson in *Reconstruction In Georgia*) it was the advance toward a greater social society. Since the transaction was a forced sale, and the price extorted, not paid willingly, it was not with Georgians to reason whether or not the 'product of reconstruction' was worth the cost."

# # # #

GEORGIA — THE CINDERELLA OF THE NINETEENTH CENTURY — 1876-1899

The Beginning of the Era of Courthouse Architecture — 1876-1900

With the state once more under the control of Georgians, the last quarter of the nineteenth century was a period of industrial growth. Mills and factories, with an influx of northern capital, were located in small towns, now connected with the ever-expanding railroad network. Raw material moved north, finished products came back on the southbound return trip.

Atlanta became the principal railhead of the Southeast, and Savannah was recognized as the chief southern port along the Atlantic seaboard.

Booming business across the nation, as the west was being won, brought about a need to control the railroads. The Interstate Commerce Act was the answer. Monopolies, huge corporations and complex financial plans — all were beyond the scope of the states, so the Federal Government provided the needed protection with the Sherman Antitrust Act. Thus the government made the first forays into the field of commerce and finance.

The Statue of Liberty, the gift of the French, was erected in New York Harbor, while out in Chicago, the Columbian Exposition sought the limelight. Not to be outdone, Atlanta was host to the Piedmont Exposition. Lucius Quintus Cincinnatus Lamar, who had been born in Putnam County, served in the Confederate Army and later became a U. S. Senator from Mississippi. He was named to the U. S. Supreme Court by President Cleveland, following the practice of Grant, to name southerners to federal positions. Mark Hanna established headquarters for William McKinley's presidential campaign in Thomasville which resulted in many northerners buying big homes and large estates in Thomas County.

The Constitution of 1877, lasting until 1945, limited the term of the governor to two years, set the membership of the State Assembly, created the office of Ordinary as the chief executive officer for the 135 existing counties, set ad valorem as the base for property taxes, and moved the Capital to Atlanta. Each county was instructed to designate a locally edited and published newspaper to be the "official" organ of the county.

The new capitol, dedicated in 1889, was built under the watchful eye of former Governor Henry D. McDaniel, who selected the architects, approved the contractors, checked the progress and kept an eye on the workmanship. When the building was finished, McDaniel still had $118.43 left of the million-dollar appropriation.

The revised public school system called for elementary schools to be available in every county, at state expense with a commissioner to be appointed by and responsible to the Governor. For the first time Justices of the Supreme Court were to be elected by popular vote.

The Georgia Institute of Technology was located in Atlanta; the State College of Agriculture and Mechanical Arts was added to the University of Georgia in Athens; the Georgia Normal and Industrial College for Women was established in Milledgeville; and an A & M College for Negroes was opened in Savannah.

Through the efforts of a young Georgia Congressman, Tom Watson, rural free mail delivery was established about the same time free home mail delivery was provided in towns with 10,000 or more population.

A wave of patriotism swept the nation following the sinking of the *USS Maine* in the harbor at Havana. In the ensuing Spanish-American War, a native Georgian was once more in the forefront of battle. General Joseph Wheeler, the famed Confederate Cavalry officer, was commissioned a Major General in the U. S. Cavalry at the age of sixty-two. He was in command of the troops that stormed San Juan Hill in the battle of Santiago de Cuba that virtually ended the war. A bespectacled "rough rider," Teddy Roosevelt, alleged to have led the charge, was so lionized by the jingo press, many Americans were led to believe he won the war single-handed.

The extent of economic stability, in the rural areas as well as the growing urban centers, was evident in the twenty-two new courthouses which were built during this period. Expanding responsibilities of county government required more office space, larger court facilities, room for the tax collector, the tax assessor, the sheriff, the coronor, the clerks and judges of the inferior, the superior and the probate courts, the Ordinary and the "county extension agent" provided by the new U. S. Department of Agriculture.

The beginning of a new era in courthouse history was seen in the new architectural approach to design as well as to form and function. Since all the courthouses were built and paid for by the county taxpayers, rivalry was keen as the new buildings took on grandeur and beauty.

It was the dawn of architectural specialists, with the firm of Morgan & Bruce designing the courthouses in Newton, Walton, Paulding, Talbot, Bulloch, Monroe, and Butts counties.

The new courthouses in Oglethorpe, Dooly, and Terrell counties were the work of W. A. Parkins, who teamed up with Bruce & Morgan to design the Hancock County Courthouse at Sparta which, with the Walton structure, are considered two of the finest examples of Victorian architecture in the South. The

Atlanta firm of Golucke & Stewart designed the Johnson, Pike, Coweta and Henry County Courthouses which are noted for the elegance of their clock towers. With the establishment of standard time, the importance of the courthouse clock lost much of its importance but none of its significance in courthouse decor.

In the beginning of the nineteenth century, Georgia had a population of 162,000 people living in twenty-four counties. At the close of the century, Georgia's population had increased tenfold to 1,837,000 in 135 counties. Of an estimated 150 courthouses built in the century, fifty-four are still in use.

#

GEORGIA — THE EMPIRE STATE OF THE SOUTH

The Dream — 1900 to 1920

With the dawn of the twentieth century, America, on the basis of the Spanish-American War, assumed a prominent role in international affairs and in Georgia came the dream — "The Empire State of the South."

Teddy Roosevelt was talking softly — he received a Nobel Prize for negotiating the end of the Russo-Japanese War. He carried a big stick — he sent the "Great White Fleet" on a two-year around-the-world cruise to show off the United States Navy. Meanwhile, Georgia supported William Jennings Bryan in 1900 and again in 1908. Alton Parker carried Georgia in 1904 and Woodrow Wilson, nominated on the forty-sixth ballot, was the choice in 1912. In 1916, Wilson received over seventy-nine percent of the vote, the highest majority Georgia had ever given a presidential candidate. In 1920, Georgians preferred James Cox to Warren Harding.

The Federal Constitution was amended to provide for the direct election of senators, establish an income tax, prohibit the manufacture, sale and transportation of alcoholic beverages and finally, let the ladies cast their own votes.

The passage of the Gold Standard Act in 1906 settled forever the debate about silver's place in the currency. Seven years later, in 1913, the Federal Reserve Act changed the banking system, establishing regulations and controls for private as well as public funds.

The Georgia Constitution was frequently amended. The Assembly set the number of counties at 145 while establishing 23 new ones. A State Highway Department was created as the Dixie Highway, crossing Georgia linked Florida with the Northeast. A court of appeals and a juvenile court were established as was a pardons and parole board. High schools became a part of the state system and compulsory schooling was enacted for children eight to fourteen, for at least four months a year. Child labor and pure food laws were passed and the state's prohibition laws made Georgia the driest state in the Union.

The Cherokee Rose became the official state flower in 1916 and Fort Pulaski was designated a National Monument by the newly organized National Park Service.

With the fading popularity of Populism, Georgia became a one-party state, although not necessarily so in presidential elections. Allen D. Candler, Joseph M. Terrell and Hoke Smith, both of the latter serving in the Senate; Joseph M. Brown, son of the Civil War governor; John M. Slaton; Nathaniel Harris, the last Confederate veteran; and Hugh M. Dorsey were governors.

In the Senate, Augustus O. Bacon, president pro tem from January, 1912 to February, 1913; William S. West, Thomas Hardwick, who would later become governor; William J. Harris; and Alexander S. Clay represented the "Peach State" as Georgia was becoming known due to the production of that crop.

Oscar Strauss, scion of the Talbot County family, became a cabinet officer when Teddy Roosevelt named him Secretary of Commerce and Labor in 1906. In 1910, President Taft appointed Joseph Rucker Lamar Associate Justice of the Supreme Court.

In the rural areas, farming was gradually changing from cotton to vegetables, fruit and grain to sustain a growing livestock industry. Textile mills moved into the smaller towns providing an adequate source of cheap labor from discouraged white sharecroppers.

In the urban centers, the trend to manufacturing and heavy industry was an open invitation to immigrate to the big cities. Electric railways replaced the horse-drawn street cars in the large cities and electric street lights were no longer a novelty. Many business houses were connected by telephones; there was an increased interest in replacing steam power with electricity. Within this era, the Georgia Railroad Commission became the Public Service Commission to regulate the power and gas companies, the street railways and the telephone exchanges.

The Gay Nineties swept away the sordid memories of the panic of 1893. In Georgia fifty-five new courthouses were built between two wars. Railroads were expanding and few were the communities not linked by rail. Rivalry sprang up between the townsfolk to build railroad depots which became status symbols.

The county unit system helped maintain a political balance of sorts between the downstate black-dominated area, the predominantly white small farmers of the mountains and the business-manufacturing elements of the cities. The county primaries took on added importance, establishing a white supremacy electorate and assuring nomination which was tantamount to election in one-party politics.

The outbreak of war in Europe in 1914 created a heavy demand for foodstuffs which started a mild boom in canning fruits and vegetables. Charles H. Herty of the staff at the University of Georgia, perfected a new method to extract turpentine from Georgia native pine and the naval stores industry became the kingpin of Georgia exports, including pitch, tar and resin.

When Congress declared war on Germany and the Central Powers in 1917, Fort McPherson which had been established near Atlanta in 1867, became the hub of wartime activities. Troops were trained at Camp Benning in Columbus, Camp Wheeler in Macon and Camp Gordon in Atlanta. Fort Screvens on Tybee Island was activated as a key in the Coastal Defense and Fort Pulaski, only recently named a National Monument by the newly-created National Park Service, was readied to house German prisoners of war. Eighty-five thousand Georgians were in the armed forces and many of them would see action before the 1918 Armistice.

Despite the arrival of the boll weevil in 1915, cotton still reigned as king, with a top price of twenty-one cents a pound. Georgians, for the first time, reset their watches and courthouse clocks as "Daylight Saving Time" was introduced to the Peach State.

From the Gay Nineties to the Roaring Twenties, Georgia's population grew from 2,216,000 in the 1900 census to 2,895,000 in 1920.

For his leadership in the war to end all wars, Woodrow Wilson was awarded a Nobel Peace Prize.

# # # #

The Goal — 1920 to 1945

The twenty-seven-year interval between the Armistice in Europe and the atom bombing of Japan opened with a return to economic normalcy in 1920, when the war machines were retooled for civilian needs. The adjustment was anything but easy: farm prices fell, the bottom dropped out of the cotton market, and the boll weevil cut production from two million bales to 600,000 within a year. Before the stock market crash in 1929, Georgia was well acquainted with depression. With the panic that followed the stock market disaster, banks failed and almost all business ground to a halt. As President Calvin Coolidge had previously remarked, "The chief business of the American people is business."

Cotton fields were fallow with many farmers able only to produce enough to feed their families. In the mountains, large scale production of frying chickens offered some hope, while the southern rural regions were turning to livestock and grain crops; there was even profit in peanuts. With credit limited, existence was a day-to-day matter on the farm as well as in the city.

The Legislature created the agricultural experiment station in Spalding County. Farmer markets were built in Atlanta, Thomasville, Macon, Tifton, Moultrie, Valdosta, and Glennville.

The 1877 Constitution was growing top-heavy with amendments as the General Assembly worked frantically to cope with the economic problems confronting the State. The Bureau of Budget was established and the Railroad Commission became the Georgia Utilities Commission. Gas tax was increased from a penny to three cents a gallon, free text books were provided in the public schools, and a department was created for the Collection of Delinquent Taxes.

With the New Deal came the State Planning Board to secure and allocate federal funds. To keep in step, new departments were created: Natural Resources, Public Safety (merged with the State Highway Patrol), Public Welfare, the Penal Administration, and Prison and Parole Commission. Abolished were the chain gang and the poll tax. The right to vote was given 18-year-olds in Georgia, the first State in the nation to lower the voting age.

The number of counties reached 159, with the merger of Campbell and Milton with Fulton and the creation of Seminole, Lanier, Brantley, Long, and Peach.

Action by the National Park Service resulted in Fort Frederica in Glynn County and the Okmulgee Indians Mounds in Bibb being named national monuments. In Cobb County, the Government purchased 20,000 acres to establish the Kennesaw Mountain National Battlefield. The Okefenokee Swamp in Ware County was designated a National Wildlife area.

In 1922, Lollie Belle Wylie and Robert Loveman teamed up to write and compose "Georgia on My Mind," which became the official state song, the brown thrasher, the state bird, and the liveoak the state tree — all by acts of the Legislature, which also urged the appointment of an "official historian" in every county.

When the Tennessee Valley Authority was created by Congress, Georgia was enriched with the Blue Ridge, Nottelly and Chatuge lakes. Along a twenty-eight mile stretch of the Tullulah and Tugaloo rivers, four hydroelectric plants were built, and Rabun County gained recreational facilities resulting from the reservoirs.

Georgians continued to vote the Democratic ticket, losing with John W. Davis in 1924 and Alfred E. Smith in 1928 but benefiting no little by voting for Franklin Delano Roosevelt in all four elections, although with diminishing support and enthusiasm.

When the old warhorse Tom Watson was elected to the United States Senate in 1920, he lived only two years to enjoy his last hurrah. Mrs. Rebecca L. Felton was named to succeed him and became the first woman to serve in the Senate. Later, two Georgians, Richard B. Russell, Jr. and Walter F. George, were to serve as President pro tem in the Senate.

From the Chattahoochee to Brasstown Bald to the Golden Isles, Georgia was surrounded by a world in convulsion, successively more violent and more inhumane. The Spanish Civil War was the prelude to Hilter's invasion of Poland in September, 1939. Diplomatic relations had been established with Stalin's Russia and Chiang Kai-shek's China, who, after overwhelming a communist rebellion, faced a menacing Japan.

At home, Margaret Mitchell's *Gone With the Wind* had sold a million copies by the time it was awarded a Pulitzer Prize; Bobby Jones retired after winning golfdom's "grand slam;" and "Tobacco Road" closed after 3,180 performances on Broadway.

Georgians became familiar with Social Security, Home Owners Loan Corporation, Civilian Conservation Corps, "SEC", "REA" and the fireside chats of FDR when they registered for the nation's first peacetime draft. The new vernacular of the Peach State included blitzkrieg, sitzkrieg, Siegfried Line, lend-lease and the pointer-and-middle-finger symbol of "victory." GI Joe fell in step with Sgt. Jasper, and Capt. Butts, and Elijah Clarke, with Robert Toombs and Joseph Wheeler, with Herschel Johnson and Alex Stevens. The grandsons of Johnny Reb and Billy Yank marched side by side to the depths of the Berlin bombshelters and to the heights of Iwo Jima.

For the fourth time in less than a century, Georgians beat their plowshares into swords. Camp Wheeler, Fort Benning and Fort Oglethorpe went into full operation, soon to be joined by Moody Air Force Base at Valdosta and Dobbins at Marietta and Warner Robins in Houston County. Hunter Army Air Field in Chatham County supported Fort Stewart in Liberty County, and Fort Gordon was very much a part of the war effort in Richmond County.

Four months after he died at Warm Springs in Meriwether County, the Japanese accepted the unconditional surrender terms of Franklin Delano Roosevelt.

As Winston Churchill prophesied — "Never in our time will life ever again be simple".

# # # #

The Realization — 1945 to 1983

The changes in Georgia, from the close of World War II in 1945 to the Semiquincentenary in 1983, were probably more radical, more over-powering and affected more people in more ways, in terms of tradition, heritage and culture than the post-Revolutionary War era and Reconstruction combined.

Scarcely had the convulsions of the war subsided when hostilities broke out in Korea, eventually engulfing the Far East and the MidEast. Hopes for peace teetertottered between the Berlin Wall and the closing of the Suez Canal, from the cold war to détente. In Georgia, all the military establishments were operating on a full-time basis. The Navy Supply School at Athens and the Marine Supply Base at Albany were newly activated as Fort Gordon became the home of the Army Signal Corps. A base for nuclear submarines was started at Kings Bay in Camden County; Dobbins Air Force Base was selected as a home for the Georgia Air National Guard.

Georgians enrolling in the Civil War Centennial Troops became a part of the State Militia as the "reenactments" included battles of the Atlanta Campaign and a three-day grand finale encampment at Fitzgerald, the town founded by and for Yankees during Reconstruction.

The extent of the political changes are seen in a new State Constitution in 1945, a consolidation and updating in 1968 and 1972, and finally with a brand new one adopted in 1982. The county unit vote, although never a part of the Constitution, was declared illegal by federal courts and abolished by the General Assembly, as was the poll tax and the chain gang.

When the United States Supreme Court ruled in 1954 that "equal but separate facilities" were illegal in the classroom, the effect was catastrophic in the surge for equal civil rights which followed. Civil rights were ruled to include social privileges in restaurants, hotels and public facilities. Public housing was desegregated and neighborhoods in suburban Georgia were integrated.

The Interstate Highway System replaced passenger trains; most counties had an airport or an airstrip; the Board of Trade and Industry replaced the Department of Commerce; and the State Highway Board became a constitutional body. For the first time in history, Georgia would elect a lieutenant governor.

Down on the farm, cotton had been deposed as king of the cash crops after one hundred twenty-five years of ruling agriculture as a tyrant. In its place were peanuts, poultry, pigs, and pine trees. Timber farming was well under way, making the most of Charles Herty's method for converting pine pulp into high grade paper products from newsprint to grocery bags. Naval stores and turpentine continued to be big business. Prosperity came to the northern hills with broiler production growing by leaps and bounds in the postwar era until Georgia led the world in poultry production. Folks were eating Georgia chicken from Hong Kong to Timbuctoo. Foreigners probably wondered how the eagle was ever selected as the official bird of America.

The signs of change were visible in every county, in every town and in every hamlet. Gone were nearly two thousand one-room schoolhouses, replaced by modern structures; each session of the General Assembly added more classrooms and hired more teachers. Down country roads, amidst a cloud of dust were hundreds of bright new yellow school buses. Governor Vandiver's administration kept the public schools open and dotted the state with National Guard armories.

The complex of the University of Georgia grew as the student body did, many making the most of federal funds under the GI Bill of Rights. The Bulldogs and the Yellow Jackets brought glory to Georgia on distant gridirons and seldom was there a bowl game that didn't have Georgia or Tech as a drawing card. Georgia Tech moved into the atomic age with a nuclear energy research reactor. With Hill-Burton funds, hospitals sprang up all over the state; few were the counties without primary medical facilities.

While the world was cheering the first men — Americans — who walked on the moon, Alaska and Hawaii were admitted to the Union; the General Assembly increased the prize to $250,000 for the first commercial oil well to be brought into production in the Peach State.

Georgians were consistent in their political philosophy with their support for Harry S Truman in his upset of Tom Dewey; they stayed with Adlai Stevenson in both of his losing battles with Ike. Then they startled the world by giving all the electoral college votes to Barry Goldwater, the first Republican candidate to every carry Georgia. Four years later, more Georgians preferred George Wallace to Hubert Humphrey or Richard Nixon. On his second time around, Georgia helped Nixon overwhelm George McGovern after John F. Kennedy carried the state in 1960. Georgia went all out for Jimmy Carter, the state's first serious presidential candidate in more than 150 years; their loyalty was still unflinching in his unsuccessful bid for a second term in 1980.

Hydroelectric dams blossomed all over the state to add pleasure to business as newly created lakes offered ideal locations for state parks, enabling Georgians to be within an hour's drive of home to these recreational areas.

Progress . . . Prosperity . . . Pride . . . accounted for thirty-four new county courthouses. Two replaced those lost by fire, the others were needed to keep pace with the growth of county business, much of it resulting from increasing home rule. Those replaced were retired to serve as community centers, museums and in some cases provide temporary space for added county business needs. In Chatham, Lumpkin DeKalb, Floyd, Haralson, Union and White counties they serve as tourist attractions.

The courthouses in Grady, Spalding and Worth counties were destroyed by fire. The courthouses in Meriwether and Fayette were restored after suffering fire damage.

Of all the original states, including some who joined the Union in the early days of the Republic, Georgia can boast of many courthouses still in full use, after a century of service and in order of seniority — Fayette, Crawford, Greene, Marion, Columbia, Burke, Thomas, Banks, Brooks, McDuffie, Clay, Pulaski, Washington, Gwinnett, Jackson, Newton, Hancock, and Walton.

Looking around — and back, we realize that Georgia is only a hundred square miles short of being as large as all of New England; that both Lakes Superior and Michigan could fit in and leave a good bit of dry land standing room.

By the end of WWII, Georgia's population had passed the three million mark; by 1970, it topped four million. By 1980, Georgia, The Empire State of The South, was home to nearly five and a half million people. The dream of James Oglethorpe became a reality.

# # # #

THE COUNTY COURTHOUSE

Does the county courthouse have any personality?

It can be the scene of happiness for the young couple applying for their marriage license; the young father registering the birth of his first child; for the elderly couple having the mortgage on their home recorded as paid in full.

To an irate taxpayer, it can be the place to grumble and growl when the day of assessment dawns.

It can be a house of horror for the prisoner convicted of a capital crime.

It may be the arena for lawyers fighting a civil case. It can be the platform of mercy for the defendant, pleading for his life. It could be the knell of doom for the man who has lost his worldly possessions in bankruptcy.

It witnesses the sobs of the sorrowful when the passing of a loved one is recorded among the death certificates.

The county courthouse may be all of this — and more.

It has been the legal center of the community, the focal point of social activity, the scene of men departing for war, the witness of those returning, the monument to those who did not.

A century ago, the courthouse may have, unwittingly, been the sight for an invading gunner's cannon, the goal of the marauding troops, who were unmindful they may have been kinfolk.

The county courthouse is the personification of its citizens.

It reflects the pride of those who planned it, built it — and paid for it. It beams down on their descendents who may pass it daily, yet seldom pause to watch the pigeons who have made the tower their home.

The balconies were the platform from which the laws and regulations and oftentimes the news were proclaimed for all to hear and heed. They were the stage for the ambitious candidate to appeal for the voter's support.

There was the day when the clock established the time for the county, autonomously, with little or no regard for what time it might be elsewhere.

If the county courthouse has a personality, it may well be vested in its being the silent witness to the birth and growth of the county, the state and, ultimately, the nation.

The courthouse is the symbol of the sovereignty of the people of that county.

# # # #

1825 to 1861

Fayetteville   *FAYETTE*   1825

This courthouse was built in 1825 at a cost of $8,000, and is the oldest courthouse in the state still in use. Legend has it that the Marquis de La Fayette was present when the cornerstone was laid. While not documented as fact, it is known that he was in Georgia about the time the building was erected. A tower was added in 1888 and a clock was placed in the tower in 1910.

When extensive renovations were made in 1965, the long center beam was removed intact and converted to a bench. Its 58-foot length is believed to be the longest single hand-hewn beam in America. Unfortunately, the courthouse was set on fire in 1982 by two men who were to be tried the following day, apparently under the delusion they could not be tried if there were no courthouse. There was serious damage to all parts of the building. A local effort raised approximately $500,000 for a complete restoration of the building. Rededication ceremonies were held on Independence Day, 1983.

Both the county and the county seat, which was created in 1821 from the Creek Cession of 1818 are named for La Fayette.

Knoxville   *CRAWFORD*   *1832*

The first courthouse in Crawford County was destroyed by fire in February 1830, and all of the records were lost. The present courthouse, begun in 1831, was built at a cost of $1,620, with a final payment of $270 made to Joseph Bemille for plastering the courtroom. The courthouse was accepted on January 25, 1832. Repairs have been made from time to time, and remodeling was done in 1965. It has a brick foundation and the exterior walls are stucco over brick masonry.

The county is named for William H. Crawford, a Georgian who served as President of the United States Senate, Minister to France, cabinet member, and candidate for the Presidency. Knoxville, the smallest county seat in Georgia, is named for General Henry Knox, an artillery officer with Washington and later a member of his Cabinet.

On the courthouse square is a monument to Joanna Troutman who designed and made the "Bonnie Blue Flag" which became the Lone Star Flag of the Texas Republic. Presentation of the flag was made to Georgia Volunteers on their way to aid in the fight for Texas independence.

Greensboro　　　　　　　　*GREENE*　　　　　　　　*1849*

The courthouse in Greensboro is unique to Georgia in several respects — it is one of the finest examples of Greek Revival architecture and the only public building of that style still in use; it is the only courthouse serving as a meeting place for the Masonic Lodge, which financed the construction of the third floor; erected in 1849 it is the third oldest courthouse still in use. The original building is brick masonry on a stone foundation. New wings were added in 1939.

The county was constituted in 1786 shortly after Georgia ratified the United States Constitution. It and the county seat are named for General Nathaniel Greene, second in command to Washington in the Continental Army. He died that same year on his plantation near Savannah, where a few years later Eli Whitney would invent the cotton gin.

Buena Vista   *MARION*   *1850*

Marion County's present courthouse, with its columned facade and clock tower, is one of the oldest and most attractive in Georgia. It was completed in 1850 at a cost of $22,500.

The first courthouse site in Marion County, selected after much discussion and delay, was at Horry, located about seven miles northeast of Tazewell, in what is now Schley County. Erected in 1828, the courthouse was a crude log cabin and, when weather permitted, court was held under the oaks surrounding the courthouse.

In 1838 the county seat was moved to Tazewell and a new courthouse and jail were erected in 1839. The courthouse burned in 1845 and all of the county records were destroyed. A new courthouse was built, at a cost of $1,637. Only one session of court was held in the building, since the people elected to move the county seat to Buena Vista, formerly known as Pea Ridge. The name was changed to commemorate the famous battle of the Mexican War. The first building in Pea Ridge is reported to have been a cake stand, followed by a general store, and three "grog" shops.

Marion County was created in 1827. It is named for the "Swamp Fox," General Francis Marion of South Carolina, a hero of the Revolution.

Appling   *COLUMBIA*   *1855*

Three years after Columbia County was constituted in 1790, the first courthouse was built. It was used until 1855 when the second and current courthouse was built at Appling, the county seat. Typical of the style of the times, John Trowbridge used brick masonry with a stucco finish and added the classic solid wood doors which are still in use.

The twelfth county to be created, Columbia was carved from Richmond County. It was settled by Quakers who were persecuted for their refusal to join in the fight for independence during the Revolutionary War. They chose to name their county for the explorer, Christopher Columbus, rather than a military hero as the surrounding new counties were being named. The county seat is named for John Appling, an original settler.

Waynesboro   **BURKE**   *1857*

Burke County, one of the eight original counties, was constituted in 1777 from the Parish of St. George. It was named for Edmund Burke, British writer, historian, and staunch defender of the colonists in their confrontations with Parliament. The county seat is named for General "Mad" Anthony Wayne.

The first courthouse in Burke was a log cabin, built in 1773. The second was a wooden structure built in Waynesboro shortly after 1777. It was destroyed by fire in 1825. A third courthouse was built in 1856 and it also was destroyed by fire. The fourth and present courthouse was built in 1857 by D.B. Plump and was financed by a $6,500 bond issue. An addition was made in 1900 and an office annex was added in 1940. The building is one of the oldest brick structures in use in Georgia. This attractive building has been completely restored at a cost of one million dollars.

Thomasville   THOMAS   *1858*

The government of Thomas County, like so many of its contemporaries, started out in a log cabin. When financial conditions warranted it, more elaborate courthouses became familiar in an evergrowing Georgia, and Thomas County was no exception.

The present courthouse, the third in the county, was built by Bowen Brothers from the design and plans of John Wind, one of Georgia's earliest known architects. The bricks, now painted white, were handmade locally. With maintenance and some additions, the building has been in continuous service since its completion in 1858, at a cost of $14,999.

When Thomas County was constituted in 1825, the state had many heroes to honor. The county and the county seat are the namesakes of General Jett Thomas, a hero in the War of 1812. Thomasville has become famous for its annual Rose Festival.

1861 to 1876

Homer   *BANKS*   *1859-65*

Banks County, created in 1858 from Franklin and Habersham counties, is named for Dr. Richard Banks who devoted a great deal of his time helping the Indians during a smallpox epidemic. The origin of the name of the county seat, Homer, has not been documented.

The courthouse, started in 1859, wasn't completed until shortly after the War Between the States. John Willis & Samuel W. Pruitt, the builders, were paid $6,600 in Confederate money.

Similar to other courthouses built during that era, it is brick masonry construction with wood double-hung windows and solid wood doors. The double stairway with the porch and overhanging eaves are distinguishing features. The courtroom contains much of the original furniture. It is also among the few "first and only" courthouses still in use.

Quitman   *BROOKS*   *1864*

The first court held in Brooks County was in the home of Thomas Folsom in January 1859. Pending the erection of the present courthouse, a small temporary courthouse was built on the lot where the Methodist Church now stands. This first courthouse was later sold to the Methodists for $1,843.75 in Confederate currency.

The contract was let in 1859 and by 1861 the building was only two-thirds completed. Due to the death of the contractor in 1862 and the scarcity of materials, the building was not finished until 1864. This courthouse is one of the few in Georgia still in use after more than 100 years. It underwent extensive remodeling and renovation in 1892 and in more recent years. The bricks were made of Brooks County clay and all of the original furniture in both the temporary and permanent courthouse was made by hand by local people.

Brooks County was created on December 11, 1858 from Thomas and Lowndes counties. It is named for Preston Smith Brooks, congressman from South Carolina and a captain in the Mexican War. The county seat was named for General John A. Quitman, a distinguished Mississippi governor and congressman.

Sandersville   *WASHINGTON*   *1869*

The first sessions of court in Washington County were held in the home of Benjamin Tennille. Later, and until 1796, court sessions were held in a log cabin in Warthen. Sandersville became the county seat in 1796. A courthouse erected at that time was a victim of the "Great Fire" of March 24, 1855, which practically destroyed the entire town.

A handsome two-story brick courthouse was built in 1856. It lay in the path of Sherman's "March to the Sea." Confederate soldiers stationed in the second story parapet fired on the invading army, killing one Union soldier and wounding eleven others. Sherman then ordered his chief of engineers to set fire to the building, destroying everything but the walls.

After the courthouse was burned in 1864, court sessions were held in the second story of a store building. Using part of the old building, the third courthouse was completed in 1869 at a cost of $22,000. The brick walls are three feet thick. In 1899 the building underwent extensive remodeling when an annex was built and a clock tower added. This serves as the present courthouse.

Created in 1784, Washington County is the namesake of George Washington. The county seat is named for a Mr. Sanders, who donated the land on which it is located.

Ft. Gaines   *CLAY*   *1871*

Clay County was constituted in 1854 from portions of Randolph and Early counties. Grand juries in 1869 and 1870 recommended that a courthouse be built. A site was purchased for $725 and the present courthouse, costing $5,000, was completed in 1871. It is the oldest courthouse in the Patula circuit and is the only courthouse resembling an antebellum plantation house.

The county is named for Henry Clay, the distinguished Kentucky statesman, often called "the Great Compromiser." The county seat was established as an outpost on the Chattahoochee River to protect the settlers against the Creek Indians. It was chartered in 1830 and named for General Edmund Gaines, who represented the government in the dealings with the Indians. In 1807, General Gaines arrested Aaron Burr, who was wanted for treason.

Lawrenceville   **GWINNETT**   *1872*

The first courts in Gwinnett were held at the home of Elisha Winn near the town of Dacula. A temporary courthouse was built in 1820 at a cost of $51 and a more permanent one was built in 1824 on land bought for a little over a dollar per acre. This building was constructed of brick and wood. The town of Lawrenceville grew up around the courthouse. In 1871 the courthouse was destroyed by fire and the grand jury, in session at the time, ordered the commissioners to rebuild on the same site. It was completed in 1872 at a cost of $6,500. It was renovated and rebuilt in 1884 and a clock tower was added around 1900. Another addition was made in 1935.

Over the years the courthouse square has had small commercial buildings at each of the corners, as a result of the commissioners deeding the corners to four attorneys in 1849, on the condition they erect a substantial fence to keep out wandering livestock. The fence they built was eight feet high with stiles on each side for people to climb over going to and from the courthouse.

Though litigation is still pending, as of this date, a Superior Court judge has ordered the commissioners to build a new courthouse.

Gwinnett County was created in 1818 and named for the famed Button Gwinnett, governor and signer of the Declaration of Independence, who was later killed in a duel with General McIntosh. The county seat is named for Captain James Lawrence who, mortally wounded on his ship in the War of 1812, gave his men the battle cry, "Don't give up the ship!"

Thomson   _McDUFFIE_   _1872_

This is the first and only courthouse erected in McDuffie County. Shortly after McDuffie was organized from Columbia and Warren counties in 1870, the courthouse was built. It was completed in 1872 at a cost of $15,000, and is still in use. In 1934 wings were added to the courthouse and the courtroom was enlarged. Substantial renovations were made in 1970 at a cost of $300,000. Elevators and stairs were added to the rear and the entire interior was refurbished.

Prior to the erection of the courthouse, the first and second stories of the Masonic building on Main Street were rented for use as a courthouse. Grand jury presentments of October 1871 state

that "As the Ordinary does not wish to take the responsibility of locating the public buildings, we appoint a committee with full power to locate and purchase a suitable site for same." The site was selected shortly thereafter and a courthouse and jail were erected.

The county is named for South Carolinian George McDuffie, who was born in Georgia, about three miles from Thomson. The county seat is named for J. Edgar Thomson who surveyed the route for the Georgia Railroad. According to legend, the State Legislature took refuge in McDuffie after the British captured Augusta, which was then the state capital.

Darien   *McINTOSH*   *1872*

The first courthouse, built seven years after McIntosh County was created in 1793, was destroyed by fire in 1864. The present courthouse of white stucco on brick masonry was built in 1872 and remodeled in 1931. Additions were built around the original structure in 1973.

The county is named for the McIntosh family, the most famous member of which was General Lachlan McIntosh, the foremost officer of the Continental Army in Georgia, who later served on Washington's staff. The origin of the name of the county seat, Darien, has not been authenticated. It was probably derived from Fort Darien, a military post established at New Inverness, the original name of the settlement given by the Scotch Highlanders.

Much of the early colonial history of this region centers around the activities of General Oglethorpe in his efforts to keep the Spanish in Florida and the French in Alabama.

Hawkinsville   **PULASKI**   *1874*

Established in 1808, Pulaski is one of the oldest counties and was a bulwark on the Indian frontier in those early years. The first county seat was Hartford, named for Nancy Hart, a spy for General Elijah Clarke, gathering information about the Tories and the British. The first courthouse was built in Hartford in 1812. Hawkinsville was named the county seat in 1836 and the first courthouse was moved across the river to the public square in Hawkinsville. In 1872 this same old wooden building was moved across the street facing the courthouse square and converted into a hotel. In the early 1890s it was moved to another location and was used as a boarding house until it was destroyed in a fire.

Pulaski's present courthouse, its second, was completed in 1874 and stands today as one of the most attractive in the state. A clock was installed in the tower in 1885 and in 1897 a handsome colonial facade was added. At that time a two-story elevation was also built to provide additional county offices. A small chapel is located just outside the courtroom. In 1910 a three-story addition, carefully planned to be harmonious with the original architectural design, was built at the rear of the building.

The county is named for Count Casimir Pulaski, a Polish nobleman killed in the siege of Savannah during the Revolution. Hawkinsville, the county seat, is named for Benjamin Hawkins, an Indian agent who helped open middle Georgia to settlement and later served in the state senate.

1876 to 1900

Jefferson   *JACKSON*   *1879*

Jackson County was created from Franklin County by an Act of February 11, 1796, making it one of the oldest of Georgia's counties. The first court convened at the home of Thomas Kirkpatrick in August 1796. Clarkesboro, in the center of the new county, was the first seat of government and a courthouse was erected there in 1799.

About 1803 the county seat was moved to Jefferson, where a log and frame courthouse was built south of the public square. A brick courthouse was built there in 1820. The present courthouse was built in 1879 at a cost of $11,112. W. W. Thomas was the architect and M. B. McGinty the builder. The clock tower was added in 1906 and interior renovations were completed in 1978. It is concrete block with masonry construction.

Jackson County is named for a Georgia Revolutionary general, James Jackson, who resigned his seat in the U. S. Senate to come back to Georgia and fight the Yazoo fraud. He later served as governor. The county seat is named for Thomas Jefferson.

It was in Jefferson that Dr. Crawford W. Long first used ether as an anesthetic during surgery in 1842.

Sparta   *HANCOCK*   *1882*

The fifteenth county in Georgia was created in 1793 from Greene and Washington counties. It is named for John Hancock whose bold signature was the first on the Declaration of Independence. Sparta, the county seat, is named for its ancient sister city in Greece as a tribute to the bravery and courage of the first settlers on the Indian frontier.

Hancock's present courthouse was begun in 1881 and the cornerstone was laid on Washington's birthday in 1882. This outstanding example of Victorian style, complete with a two-tiered clock tower, is the work of architects Parkins & Bruce. James Smith was the builder, with funds furnished by David Dixon who carried the keys to the courthouse in his pocket until the loan was paid in full.

The first court was held at a little weather-boarded store known as "Four Mile Store," which is still in existence. The first courthouse, a wooden structure, was erected where the old jail now stands. A two-story brick structure was built later and was subsequently torn down in 1881 to allow the present courthouse to be built on the same site.

Monroe   *WALTON*   *1883*

An early Georgia county, Walton County was created in 1818 from the Creek Cession and is named for George Walton, one of Georgia's signers of the Declaration of Independence.

Soon after the county was set up, court was held in a cowbarn in appropriately named Cowpens. Monroe, named for President James Monroe, became the county seat in 1821. Court was held in temporary buildings until the first courthouse was completed in 1823, on land donated by Elisha Butts. This modest structure was used until 1845, when another courthouse was erected.

The third and present courthouse was designed by Bruce & Morgan with James Smith & Company doing the construction for $23,865. Built in 1883, the courthouse, like many of its counterparts, is brick masonry with limestone decoration and has a unique one-story porch over the entrance. The clock tower was added in 1910. Restoration in 1933 cost $28,000 and since then additions have augmented the beauty of the building.

Covington **NEWTON** *1884*

The Newton County Courthouse was designed by architects Bruce & Morgan and built by James Smith & Company in 1884. It is characteristic of the era, constructed of brick masonry with stone decoration.

The first court was held in a log cabin at Brickstore with Judge Clayton presiding. The cabin, 60 by 20 feet, was completed in 1822 at a cost of $50, not counting the $12 that was paid to James Kilpatrick for clearing off the public square. The second courthouse was a two-room log building erected on the same site. It burned on December 31, 1883. The present handsome building was then erected.

The county is named for Sgt. John Newton, a companion of Revolutionary hero Sgt. William Jasper. The county seat was first named Newtonboro, but was later called Covington after another soldier of the Revolution, Leonard Covington.

Cuthbert   _RANDOLPH_   _1886_

In Randolph County, as in most early counties in Georgia, court sessions were held in the homes of prominent citizens until a courthouse and a jail could be erected. The first courthouse was a crude wooden building which was erected in 1837 on the public square at a cost of $1 220. The second courthouse was a brick structure, also built on the public square, and completed in 1840. It was torn down in 1886 to make way for a Confederate monument. At that time the present courthouse was built at a cost of $19,500. It is an attractive building with the usual steeple and clock tower common to courthouses of this era. The architects were Kimball, Wheeler & Parkins.

The county was carved from Lee County in 1828. It is named for John Randolph, the famed Virginia statesman, who had regained the favor he lost in Georgia when the original Randolph County was changed to Jasper. The county seat is named for John A. Cuthbert, editor and jurist, who gained immortality as a result of a fistfight at the state capitol over the Indian removal issue. Lumpkin was the first county seat of Randolph but became the county seat of Stewart when that county was created. The county seat of Randolph was then moved to Cuthbert.

Milledgeville   *BALDWIN*   *1887*

The first courthouse in Baldwin County was a log cabin in Hillsborough where court was held from 1806 to 1808. Hillsborough became a part of Putnam County in 1807 and the county seat was moved to Milledgeville, where court sessions were held in the state capitol. The first courthouse in Milledgeville was built in 1814 at a cost of $3,975. It was replaced by a more spacious building in 1847, which was destroyed by fire in 1861. Another courthouse was begun in 1885 and completed in 1887. This courthouse was remodeled and enlarged in 1937 and again in 1965. It is still in use today. During intervals when there was no courthouse, court sessions were held in the legislative chamber, the Masonic lodge and the old Opera House.

Baldwin County was created in 1803 and named for Abraham Baldwin, signer of the U. S. Constitution from Georgia and known as the "father" of the University of Georgia. The county seat is named for John Milledge, war hero, governor of Georgia, and donor of most of the original lands owned by the University of Georgia in Athens.

Lexington　　　　　　　　*OGLETHORPE*　　　　　　　　*1887*

Georgia's nineteenth county was created in 1793 from Wilkes County and honors James Oglethorpe, the founder of the Colony. The Act creating the county provided that "The justices of the Inferior Court of Oglethorpe County may contract for the building of a courthouse and jail, and may raise by tax, not exceeding two hundred and fifty pounds for this purpose." Pursuant to this authorization, a courthouse was erected at Philomath. A second courthouse was built in 1819. The present courthouse was erected in 1887 for $30,000 by W. W. McAfee and R. E. Bondurant from plans by L. B. Wheeler, W. H. Parkins and H. I. Kimball. The exterior walls are locally made brick; the arches are constructed of granite from a nearby quarry; the trim is Ollitic limestone; and the wood is from local timber. The Seth Thomas clock in the tower weighs half a ton.

The county seat is Lexington, commemorating the battle where the "shot was fired that was heard around the world."

Home of some of the most distinguished families in Georgia, six Georgia counties have been named for residents of Oglethorpe County.

Vienna   **DOOLY**   *1892*

One of the earliest counties, Dooly was created in 1821 from the Creek Indian land cession. It honors Colonel John Dooly who was murdered in his home by a band of roving Tories. Vienna, originally called Centerville, is named for the Austrian capital and was home of Walter F. George, distinguished jurist and United States senator who also served as president pro tem of the U. S. Senate.

The first county seat was the small town of Berrien, named for Senator Berrien. When the people became angry with the Senator, the name of the town was changed to Drayton. In 1839 the county seat was moved to Vienna.

Dooly County has had four courthouses, three in Vienna and one at Drayton. The first courthouse in Vienna was a wooden structure which was destroyed by fire on May 1, 1847. A wooden courthouse was erected in 1849 and was later torn down to make way for the present courthouse. It was designed by W. A. Parkins and built by J. P. Heard for $25,000. Constructed of Georgia granite and brick which was made on the site, the building houses the original vault. Installed in 1892, it was patented by Victor Safe & Lock Company and is still in use. The most recent renovations to the building were completed in 1963.

Dallas   PAULDING   *1892*

The first courthouse in Dallas was a victim of fire. The present structure, completed in 1892, was designed by Bruce & Morgan and built by G. M. Roberts. It is primarily Queen Anne style with colored glass windows in the tower. Extensive renovations were made in 1956.

One of the twenty-three Georgia counties carved from the original Cherokee County, Paulding County was created in 1832. It is named for John Paulding, one of the soldiers who helped capture the British spy Major André, an accomplice of Benedict Arnold. The first county seat, Van Wert, was named for Isaac Van Wert, a companion of Paulding. The town no longer exists and its location is uncertain. Dallas, the present county seat, honors George M. Dallas, vice-president during the Polk administration.

Talbotton   **TALBOT**   *1892*

As in most counties, the Commissioners appointed to select a site and build a courthouse had a difficult time pleasing the inhabitants. Many wanted the courthouse to be located in the town of Centerville, but the commissioners chose a more central location, laid it off and named it Talbotton.

Court business was first held in the home of Robert Brooks and perhaps other places. A substantial brick courthouse was built in 1831. It was said to be "large and well arranged." This building was destroyed by fire in February 1892 and replaced by the present courthouse. It was built by W. B. Bennett of Barnesville for a total cost of $17,000. It is typical of the courthouses built in this area and one of the many designed by Bruce & Morgan. The Supreme Court of Georgia met in the courtroom in April 1981 to commemorate the 135th anniversary of the first session of the court held in Talbotton in 1846.

Both the county, created in 1827, and the county seat are named in honor of Governor Matthew Talbot. Talbotton was the first home in America of Lazarus Straus. Under the leadership of his sons, Oscar, Nathan and Isador, Macy's became one of the world's most prestigious department stores.

Dawson   **TERRELL**   *1892*

Terrell County was organized from Randolph and Lee counties in 1856, and the first courthouse was built in Dawson in 1857. The second and present courthouse was completed in 1892 at a cost of $36,832. It is "high-Victorian" style and was designed by architect William Parkins. J. B. Sample was the builder.

The county is named for Dr. William Terrell of Sparta, state legislator and congressman, who died in 1855. Dawson is named for William C. Dawson, a jurist and United States Senator.

A refugee camp was set up in Dawson to give shelter to 300 women and children who had fled Atlanta in 1864.

Statesboro   **BULLOCH**   *1894*

One of the oldest counties in Georgia, Bulloch County was created from Bryan and Screven counties in 1796. Beginning in May 1797, Superior Court was held, either at private homes or outside under the trees. The first courthouse was a wooden structure built around 1800. About 1807 a second courthouse was built. It was destroyed by Sherman's army in 1864, and was replaced by a two-story wooden courthouse, which was later moved down the street and became known as "The Opera House."

The present building was erected in 1894. Bruce & Morgan designed the Queen Anne structure, which was later painted white. John McKenzie was the builder. The courthouse was financed by the sale of town lots and private contributions. The outside walls are brick masonry with painted plaster interior walls. This building was renovated in 1914, and has been modernized inside.

Bulloch County is named for Archibald Bulloch, Revolutionary leader who presided over the Provincial Congress in July 1775. He became Georgia's provisional Governor in 1776 and died mysteriously in office in 1777.

"Statesborough" was chartered in December 1803 on a two-hundred acre tract donated to Bulloch County for a county seat. It is thought that the name was in honor of the fight for states rights. In 1866 the town was chartered as a city and the spelling changed to Statesboro.

Elberton   **ELBERT**   *1894*

Elbert County's present courthouse is a two-story brick building that was erected in 1894. Its cupola tower is reminiscent of the old state capitol in Williamsburg, Virginia. One of the most distinctive of Georgia's courthouses, it features native granite for which the region is internationally known. The building was designed by Hunt & Lamm and built by L. L. Stevenson for $35,000. It was extensively renovated in 1964.

The first courthouse was a two-story frame building which was erected in 1800. According to county records, the first Superior Court was held at the home of T. A. Carter in January 1791, with Judge Walton presiding.

Elbert County was created from a portion of Wilkes County in 1790. Both the county and the county seat are named for Revolutionary War General Samuel Elbert, who later served as governor.

Elbert County was the home of the famous and courageous Revolutionary spy, Nancy Hart, who "disposed" of six Tories during the War. It was also the home of Reverend Daniel Tucker, who inspired the song "Old Dan Tucker."

The old town of Petersburg, at the junction of the Broad and Savannah rivers, was once considered as a possible site of the State Capital. At that time it was the third largest town in Georgia.

Oglethorpe　　　　　　　　　*MACON*　　　　　　　　　*1894*

Macon County has had only two courthouses, the first built in 1837 shortly after the county was organized, and the present courthouse which was completed in May 1894. The first one was destroyed by fire in 1857. The present courthouse is brick masonry on a concrete foundation. Built by Wagner & Gorenflo, there is no record of who designed the building. It is crowned with two castle-like cupolas which complement the clock tower, a requisite of the era in which it was built.

The county is named for Nathaniel Macon, a North Carolina statesman who served as president pro tem of the U. S. Senate. Oglethorpe, the county seat, is named for the founder of the Georgia colony. The first county seat was the little town of Lanier, now extinct. The county seat was moved to Oglethorpe in 1854 to be on the railroad. A move to change the county seat to Montezuma in 1893 was defeated. Nearby Marshallville used to boast that it had "no lawyer, no Yankee, no motion picture house or jail."

Camp Sumter, at Andersonville, where 12,000 Union prisoners died, is located in Macon County. It was also in Macon County where Sam Rumph developed the Elberta peach, the foundation of the state's peach industry.

Wrightsville   *JOHNSON*   *1895*

The present Johnson County courthouse is a brick masonry building with stone decoration. It was built on the public square in 1895 and renovations were made in 1938. Designed by Golucke & Stewart and built by Wagner & Gorenflo, it is unique in that its "Y" floor plan provides for no main entrance.

The county was created in 1858 from portions of Emanuel, Laurens and Washington counties. The first courthouse was a wooden structure built in 1859.

Johnson County is named for Georgia statesman Herschel V. Johnson, an unsuccessful vice-presidential candidate on the Douglas ticket against Abraham Lincoln in 1860. He later became a U. S. Senator and governor of Georgia. Wrightsville, the county seat, is named for a pioneer resident, John B. Wright. Lately it has become famous as the home of another Herschel, an outstanding football player.

Zebulon   *PIKE*   *1895*

When Pike County was organized in 1822, the little town of Newnan, located about one mile west of the present town of Meansville, was selected as the county seat. The first courthouse, constructed of hewn logs, was built there. At that time Newnan was in the center of Pike County. When Upson County was carved from Pike, Newnan was left too far from the center of the remaining county and it soon passed from existence as a town. In 1824 another county seat was selected and named Zebulon. A brick courthouse was built on the public square at a cost of $8,000.

The present courthouse was erected on the same site in 1895. It features a small columned portico over the first floor entrance and a four-sided clock tower, typical of the era. Arthur Marshall was paid $18,200 for constructing the building which was designed by Golucke & Stewart.

Both the county and the county seat are named for General Zebulon M. Pike, discoverer of Pike's Peak in Colorado. He was killed in Canada during the War of 1812.

Homerville   *CLINCH*   *1896*

The first court and election in Clinch County were held in the home of Jonathan Knight in 1850. The first courthouse for Clinch County was built in 1852. It burned in 1856. A second courthouse was erected in 1859 and it also was destroyed by fire in 1867. The present courthouse is a two-story brick structure with a slate roof. It was built in 1896 by T. J. Darling at a cost of $6,686.28. The building was substantially renovated in 1936. The first courthouse was moved to a station on the old Atlantic & Gulf Railway and a town grew up around it. Incorporated in 1869, the town was called Homerville in honor of Dr. John Homer Mattox, who laid out the town on property which he owned.

Clinch County was created in 1850 from parts of Lowndes and Ware counties and named in honor of Duncan L. Clinch, congressman and general. The first county seat, with the beautiful name of Magnolia, has long since vanished from the map.

Forsyth   MONROE   *1896*

Monroe County was organized in 1821 and the first session of Superior Court was held on June 3, 1822 at the home of H. H. Lumpkin, nine miles northwest of Forsyth. The first county seat was Johnstonville, established in 1821, but there is no record of a courthouse there. The first courthouse was built in the center of the public square in Forsyth in 1825. This sturdy old building served until it was torn down and the present two-story brick courthouse erected in 1896 on the same site, on a foundation of granite rock. It is typical of the courthouses built in this era — red brick, slate roof and an imposing clock tower. The contractor was the Knoxville Building Company from plans by Bruce & Morgan. The Monroe *Advertiser* on November 24, 1896 proudly

proclaimed, "It is magnificent in every appointment, cost nearly $30,000 and is paid for."

Monroe County is named for President James Monroe. The county seat is a memorial to John Forsyth, who, while serving as minister to Spain, pulled off one of the greatest real estate deals of all time when he negotiated the purchase of Florida from Spain in 1819.

The first railroad in Georgia was built in 1834 connecting Forsyth and Macon.

One of the last battles of the War Between the States was fought in Monroe County on April 19, 1865, the same day that Lincoln's funeral train departed from Washington on its way to Springfield, Illinois.

66

McDonough   *HENRY*   *1897*

Henry County is one of the seventeen counties created from the Creek Indian land cessions. The first courthouse was a temporary one erected in 1823. A second courthouse was built shortly after this but, according to records, was sold and replaced by the present structure. This imposing courthouse was completed around 1897. Following Romanesque lines, it is brick on masonry construction with metal and wood cornice. Designed by Golucke & Stewart, it was built by Frank P. Heifner for $13,794.48. It is not in the center of town "on the square" as were most courthouses that were built during this era.

Henry County is named for the Virginia patriot Patrick Henry who cried "Give me liberty or give me death!" McDonough, the county seat, developed at the site of a prominent Indian trading post honors James McDonough, a naval captain who defeated the British fleet on Lake Champlain during the War of 1812.

Nashville　　　　　　　*BERRIEN*　　　　　　　*1898*

The first courthouse in Berrien County was a log schoolhouse. A two-story wooden courthouse was built in 1858. It served the needs of the county until 1898, when the present courthouse was built on the same public square. Built by Hager & Winston from plans by W. Chamberlain & Co., it has a concrete foundation with brick masonry walls. Windows are wood double-hung and the interior walls are plaster. The original cost of the building was $17,000. The clock tower is one of its most outstanding features.

Berrien County was created from Coffee, Irvin and Lowndes counties in 1856. It is named for U. S. Senator John MacPherson Berrien, who was also a justice of the Supreme Court of Georgia. The county seat is named for Revolutionary War hero General Francis Nash, for whom the Tennessee capital is also named.

Jackson   **BUTTS**   *1898*

The first courthouse in Butts County was nearing completion in 1818 when it was destroyed by fire. Another courthouse was built and was used until 1860, when another one was erected. The present courthouse was built by J. H. McKenzie & Sons, with Bruce & Morgan, the architects, in 1898 at a cost of $24,980. The walls are brick masonry with a concrete block foundation. The interior walls are plaster and the hall floors are marble.

Butts County was created from parts of Henry and Monroe counties in 1825. It is named for Captain Samuel Butts of the Georgia militia, who was killed at the Battle of Chillabee in 1814. The county seat is named for Andrew Jackson.

Robert Grier, astronomer and founder of *Grier's Almanac* lived with his family near the community of Stark, where he is buried.

Jonesboro   *CLAYTON*   *1898 — 1962*

Scarcely had Clayton County set up a government when it was hit by the full force of the Sherman juggernaut in 1864. The first courthouse was a small wooden structure built in 1859 and destroyed during the Battle of Jonesboro. Another courthouse was built in 1869. It is still standing and is used as the Jonesboro Masonic Lodge. The third courthouse was completed in 1898 and is presently used for county offices. Bond issues for this courthouse were defeated in 1896 and 1897, so in 1898 the commissioners increased the levy from 1 1/2 mills to 10 and paid cash for the building. In 1962 a new courthouse was erected adjacent to and almost surrounding the older structure whose tower is still visible.

Clayton County was formed in 1858 and named for Judge Augustin S. Clayton, a prominent Georgia statesman. The county seat, which was originally called Leaksville, was changed to Jonesboro when the Central Railroad reached there. The name change honored Captain Samuel C. Jones, who surveyed the line for the railroad.

1900 to 1920

Ellaville   *SCHLEY*   *1900*

The Schley County Courthouse, designed by Golucke & Stewart and built by Algernon Blair in 1900, prompted the county historian to write "with pride the citizens of Schley County viewed its architectural beauty and the splendid workmanship displayed in its erection."

The county was created in 1857 from Marion and Sumter counties and is named for William Schley, judge, congressman and governor. The first courthouse was built the following year. In 1885 an enterprising editor set up his press in the courthouse and there is no doubt that it was the "official organ" of the county. In 1898 the Grand Jury condemned the building, recommending that a new one be built. After much deliberation, the commissioners voted to issue $15,000 in bonds for that purpose.

The building was completed in the spring of 1900. The gables, steeple and clock tower are typical of the rural courthouses built during this era.

The county seat, near Pond Town, was relocated in 1859. It was named for Miss Ella Burton, daughter of one of the pioneer families who settled the county.

Danielsville   *MADISON*   *1901*

Madison County, named for President James Madison, outgrew two frame courthouses. The present structure is located on the public square in Danielsville, as were the first two courthouses. It was designed by J. W. Golucke and completed by Fred Wagner in 1901 at a cost of $22,500. The bricks were made locally from river bottomland clay. It was reported that G. O. Griffeth had the contract to furnish sand for the courthouse and that it would "take him about seventy days with one hand hauling ten loads a day to furnish enough."

Madison County, the 38th county, was created from Clarke, Elbert, Franklin, Jackson and Oglethorpe counties in 1811. The county seat was named for General Allen Daniel who donated the land on which the county buildings were located. Dr. Crawford W. Long, who discovered the use of ether as an anesthetic for pain, was born in Danielsville two years before it was incorporated in 1817.

Moultrie　　　　　　*COLQUITT*　　　　　　*1902*

In 1859 the Legislature designated a 50-acre tract of land as Moultrie, the county seat. A sizeable rough-hewn log structure was built for a courthouse. That structure burned in 1881, destroying nearly all of the valuable records. A two-story frame building was erected but leaders warned that it was a fire trap and should be replaced. A bond election for a new courthouse failed in 1901. The commissioners then levied a tax to cover the cost of a courthouse which was completed in 1902 at a cost of $29,500, including the cost of a secondhand clock. It was paid for in three years. This is one of the few courthouses built of Georgia marble. It reflects the workmanship of J. H. Harris, G. W. Milligan, and the A. J. Bryan Company. There have been several moves to replace the old building but it was decided to completely renovate it in 1956-57 at a cost of $285,000. The jail which complements the courthouse is considered a masterpiece of contemporary penal institutions.

The county was created in 1856 from Thomas and Lowndes counties and is named for Walter T. Colquitt, congressman, judge, and U. S. Senator. The county seat is named for General William Moultrie, a hero of the Revolution.

Bainbridge   *DECATUR*   *1902*

There is an aura of the sea in Bainbridge, Georgia's first modern inland port. The county, created in 1823 from portions of Early County, is named for Commodore Stephen Decatur, a hero of the war with the pirates of Tripoli, later killed in a duel. The county seat is named for Commodore William Bainbridge, a one-time commander of "Old Ironsides." There has been a settlement at the site of Bainbridge since 1810. Called Fort Hughes, it served as a base for General Andrew Jackson in the Seminole War.

The courthouses kept pace with the growth of the county. A wooden courthouse was erected in 1824. It was replaced by a more substantial brick courthouse in 1832. Another larger brick structure was built in 1855 and served the county until 1902, when the present courthouse was built.

Algernon Blair designed the classic facade and gave the building its distinctive campanile, an innovation for that era. Nicholas Ittner was paid $34,500 for the construction. A jail was added later.

Crawfordville   *TALIAFERRO*   *1902*

Taliaferro, constituted in 1825 from five adjoining colonial frontier counties, memorializes Colonel Benjamin Taliaferro who served during the Revolutionary War.

The county seat, Crawfordville, was named for statesman and diplomat William H. Crawford, a one-time candidate for President. Liberty Hall, a state shrine, is in Crawfordville. It was the home of Alexander H. Stephens, Vice-President of the Confederacy.

The county has had two courthouses, both of them brick. The first was built in 1828 and served the needs of the county until 1901, when it was torn down to make way for the present courthouse. It was designed by Lewis F. Goodrich and built by John H. McKenzie & Sons. County officials estimated the cost of the building at $19,600 while $10,000 was considered sufficient by the taxpayers. As a compromise, 600,000 bricks, several tons of granite and a couple of thousand board-feet of lumber were used from the 1828 courthouse in the new one.

The High Victorian style is unusual in that the clock tower is located at the corner of the building, rather than the center. It is visible for miles in the picturesque countryside typical of this fertile region of the state.

Reidsville   *TATTNALL*   *1902*

Thirty-one years after Tattnall County was carved from Montgomery County, the first courthouse, a log cabin, was built. It was replaced in 1854. The present two-story brick courthouse was built in 1902. Designed by J. W. Golucke, the construction costs were $60,000. In 1964 the towers were removed during an extensive remodeling and the appearance of the building changed from Georgian to Federalist.

The original county seat of Tattnall was on the Ohoopee River near Drake's Ferry. In 1828 a committee was named to select a site for a courthouse at the geographical center of the county. When a post office opened there in 1832 the site was named Reidsville. Some sources say it derives its name from a low point on the courthouse square were reeds grew, although the spelling is different. Other sources indicate the town is named for Superior Court Judge Robert E. Reid, who became a Territorial Governor of Florida.

The county is named for an early Georgia governor, Josiah Tattnall, who, when he was Governor, signed a bill restoring citizenship to his father, a Tory who fled to England rather than fight against England.

Cartersville   *BARTOW*   1903

Bartow County was created from Cherokee County in 1832. It was originally called Cass County and the county seat was known as Cassville. First named to honor General Lewis Cass of Michigan, his views on slavery brought him disrepute. The name was changed in 1861 to honor Colonel Francis Stebbins Bartow, who was killed at the first battle of Manassas. His last words were said to be, "They have killed me boys, but never give up." One of the first sessions of the Supreme Court of Georgia was held in Cassville.

After the courthouse in Cassville was destroyed by Sherman, the county seat was moved and named in honor of Farish Carter, one of the largest landowners in antebellum Georgia. A new courthouse was built in 1873 but proved to be highly unsatisfactory due to the noise of passing trains. The structure still stands and is presently used as a warehouse.

A new site on higher ground was selected as a more serene site for county business. The present courthouse was completed in 1903. It is another of the J. W. Golucke & Associates neoclassical designs, featuring the clock tower and pillored entrance. The dependable Fred Wagner was selected as the contractor. The building has a stone foundation with brick masonry walls. The interior walls are painted plaster.

Bartow County was the home of Rebecca L. Felton, the first woman to serve in the United States Senate. The Etowah Indian Mounds are a popular tourist attraction in the county.

Greenville   **MERIWETHER**   *1903*

The first courthouse in Meriwether County was a handsome, two-story brick structure, completed in 1832. It was severely damaged by a tornado in 1893, but, after repairs, continued in use until it was razed to make way for the present courthouse.

Built in 1903, this courthouse was considered one of the finest in the state, an outstanding example of classical revival architecture. Designed by J. W. Golucke, it was constructed by W. M. McAfee for $28,000. On January 27, 1976, the building burned. An entirely new interior was constructed within the original walls. The cost of the restoration, completed in 1980, was $1,900,000.

In 1827 the Legislature authorized Meriwether County from land in Troup County which had been part of the Creek Cession. David Meriwether, Revolutionary soldier, congressman and Speaker of the Georgia House is honored with the legendary General Nathanial Greene, for whom the county seat is named.

Blackshear   *PIERCE*   *1903*

The first Pierce County Courthouse was built in 1858, the year after the county was formed from portions of Appling and Ware counties. Located at the corner of Main Street and South Central Avenue in Blackshear, it served as a Confederate hospital during the War Between the States. The building was destroyed by fire in 1875 and most of the county records were lost.

The second courthouse was erected on Park Street in 1875. It was replaced by the present courthouse in 1903. It is another design of J. W. Golucke's and was built for $19,974 by George A. Clayton. Only two columns support the portico entrance, possibly the result of the need to stay within the budget.

The county is named for President Franklin Pierce. The county seat is the namesake of General David Blackshear, who fought in the Indian Wars after service in the War of 1812.

Jeffersonville   *TWIGGS*   *1903*

Twiggs County, created from Wilkinson County in 1809, was named for Revolutionary War hero General John Twiggs. The county seat honors a local family.

In 1810 a lot was selected as the county seat and the town of Marion was established. The first courthouse was completed in 1812. It was a large two-story building with eight entrances. The town grew and prospered and soon claimed one thousand residents. As in many towns of the era, residents refused to allow the railroad to come to Marion. It was connected to Macon instead. Marion gradually withered and the county seat was moved to Jeffersonville in 1868. Marion eventually disappeared from the map.

The Marion courthouse was dismantled and moved by oxcart to the site of the present building. Following a disastrous fire in 1901, J. W. Golucke, the architect, teamed up with Fred Wagner to build the new edifice for $30,000.

Jesup **WAYNE** *1903*

Wayne County was created in 1803 from the Creek Cession of 1802. The selection of a county seat was certainly not a matter of snap judgment nor one made in haste. It was not until 1829 that the commissioners finally selected a site one mile from the town of Waynesville as a place for the public buildings of Wayne County. As late as 1849 court was held in "The Academy." By 1860 a courthouse had been erected and it was described as "a small frame building in the woods nine miles northwest of Waynesville."

A more central location, Jesup, was decided upon when Charlton County was formed from Wayne in 1855, leaving Waynesville in the extreme lower part of the county. The courthouse built there was replaced in 1903 by the present building. Costing $12,500, it was designed by S. A. Baker and built by T. J. Darling. The building is traditional in style, although the four-faced clock is unique.

The county, and original county seat, honors General "Mad" Anthony Wayne, one of the most colorful characters of the Revolutionary War. The present county seat was incorporated in 1870 and was named for the Indian fighter, General Jesup.

Abbeville   *WILCOX*   *1903*

The first courthouse in Wilcox County was a wooden structure built in 1858. It was destroyed by fire after many years of use.

The second and present building was completed in 1903, in an era when counties vied for architectual beauty in the new courthouses. The design of Frank P. Milburn was selected and J. H. McKenzie was awarded the construction contract. It features an octagonal baroque-styled dome with a lantern and a clock tower boasting four clocks — one on each side of the tower. The building itself is brick masonry with stone accents and has three floors, unusual for that time.

Created from sections of Dooly, Irwin, and Pulaski counties, records show the county is the namesake of Captain John Wilcox. Other authorities indicate it is named for General Mark Wilcox, one of the legislators who strongly advocated creation of the Georgia Supreme Court. The county seat is named for the Abbeville District of South Carolina.

Washington   **WILKES**   *1903*

Wilkes, one of Georgia's original counties, is extraordinary in several respects. Created by the Constitution of 1777, it was never an Anglican Parish as were the others, having been established from both Cherokee and Creek land cessions. It honors John Wilkes, a member of Parliament who was a champion of freedom for the Colonies. Washington, the county seat, is the first city in the nation to be named in honor of George Washington. Wilkes County has been the birthplace or residence of many prominent Georgians, including ten governors: Heard, Clarke, Talbot, Early, Lumpkin, Rabun, Towns,

Ware, Forsyth and Matthews.

The first courthouse in the county was built in 1785. The present courthouse was erected in 1903. It was a resplendent building complete with an ornate clock tower and featuring Romanesque arches over the doors and windows. The structure was designed by Frank P. Milburn and built by the Savannah Contracting Company. Following a devastating fire in December, 1958, the building was reconstructed, but the beautiful old clock was not replaced.

Newnan   *COWETA*   *1904*

Coweta County was created by Acts of June 9, 1825 and December 11, 1826 from lands ceded by the Creek Indians. It is named for the Cowetas, a tribe of the Lower Creek Indians. The county seat is named for General Daniel Newnan, noted Indian fighter and U. S. Congressman.

The original seat of government was at Bullsboro, located about two-and-one-half miles northeast of Newnan. The Inferior Court of the county selected the present site of Newnan for the county seat and the first courthouse was built in 1829. It was a two-story brick structure, fronted by four white Doric columns on the west side. This courthouse served as a hospital during the War Between the States and was shelled by federal artillery. The building served until 1904 when it was demolished after the March Term of Court to make way for the present courthouse.

The architect, J. W. Golucke, considered this courthouse his most ambitious project. Formally opened on December 30, 1904, the structure was built by R. D. Cole Manufacturing Company for $56,998. It is a fine example of Neo-Greek Revival architecture. The interior of the courthouse was remodeled in 1974.

Louisville   *JEFFERSON*   *1904*

Jefferson County, memorializing Thomas Jefferson, was very prominent in early Georgia history. The year it was created, 1796, was the year the state capital was moved to Louisville, so named in honor of the French king, Louis XVI. It was here that all records of the Yazoo land frauds were ignited by sunrays through a magnifying glass, as though "fire from the heavens."

Louisville served as Georgia's capital until 1806, when it was replaced by Milledgeville. It wasn't until 1816 that the first of several courthouses was built. During the interim, court was held in private residences, the Louisville Academy, the Old Coffee House, and the old State Capitol building.

For $1,500, the county purchased the Capitol building to be used as a courthouse, with the Masonic Lodge retaining use of the upper floor. At that time, the original courthouse was sold for $100 to a group for use as a church. Offerings at the church were apparently slim since the building was repossessed eight years later and sold again for $100.

A new courthouse, using much of the material from the Capitol building, was completed in 1848 at a cost of $6,000. It served until the present structure was built on the same foundation in 1904. The contractor, F. P. Heifner, built it for $37,615. The neoclassic design of W. F. Denny is typical of courthouse architecture of the early twentieth century.

Valdosta　　　　　*LOWNDES*　　　　　*1904-5*

Lowndes County has perhaps had more courthouses and county seats than any other county in Georgia.

The first courthouse was built in 1828 at Franklinsville, the first county seat. It was constructed of hewn logs and cost $215. This courthouse was torn down and moved to Lowndesville when the county seat was moved there in 1833. In 1834 a second courthouse was erected. The county seat was then moved to Troupville, where the third courthouse was built in 1842. It burned in 1858 and in 1859 the county seat was moved to the new town of Valdosta. The fourth courthouse was soon erected at the corner of Central Avenue and Ashley Streets. A fire destroyed most of the building in 1869 and the fifth courthouse was erected on the public square in 1871. A sixth courthouse, constructed of red brick and enclosed by an iron fence, was built in 1875.

The present courthouse, the seventh, was erected in 1905. It was designed by Frank P. Milburn and built for $60,000 by Algernon Blair. A new annex was added in 1962.

The county, created in 1825, honors a distinguished statesman of South Carolina, the Honorable William Lowndes, once nominated for President by the Legislature. Valdosta was named for the country estate of Governor Troup in Laurens County, which in turn was named for an Alpine valley called Val d' Osta, said to antedate Rome some 450 years.

Hazelhurst   *JEFF DAVIS*   *1905*

The present Jeff Davis courthouse is the only one to serve the county, since it was not created until 1905, making it one of the youngest counties in the state. It is the first courthouse in Georgia built of concrete blocks with a stucco finish. The design of W. Chamberlain Company was completed by M. T. Lewman in 1905 at a cost of $24,351. It was extensively renovated in 1975. The imposing structure is distinctive for its fortress-like rounded towers which blend with the traditional clock tower.

There was considerable sentiment to name the county for Judge John A. Cromartie of Hazelhurst, but the Legislature refused to change its policy not to name new counties for living persons. Jefferson Davis, Secretary of War, Senator and President of the Confederacy was the choice of the lawmakers. The county seat is named for the civil engineer who surveyed the route of the Macon & Brunswick Railroad which passed through the area.

Gray   *JONES*   *1905*

Jones County, named for James Jones, Savannah member of the Georgia House and later congressman, was created from a part of Baldwin County in 1807. The county seat was Albany, a tiny hamlet where court was held at the home of William Jones. Two years later, Albany was renamed Clinton and a temporary structure served as the courthouse until 1816 when a permanent facility was erected.

Refusing the coming of the railroad, the citizens of Clinton saw the rails, as well as trade and settlers move a mile north to Gray, a town named for a family of early settlers. In 1905, the county seat also moved to Gray. A new brick courthouse, still in use, and noted for its beautiful arched clock tower, was designed by J. W. Golucke and built for $35,000 by the Atlanta Fireproofing Company.

Morgan County's courthouse, on a corner facing the public square, is one of the most imposing in the state. It is of the "Y" or triangular design as contrasted to the square or cross design and is capped with a majestic clock tower. Designed by Atlanta architect J. W. Golucke, it was built in 1905 by Winder Lumber Company.

The first courthouse was a large red brick square building erected in 1809 on the public square in the center of Madison. When the present courthouse was built it was converted to an office which was destroyed by fire in 1917.

Morgan County, created from Baldwin County in 1807, is named for Revolutionary General Daniel Morgan and the county seat for President James Madison. A Georgia historian wrote in 1845 that "Madison is the wealthiest and most aristocratic village on the stagecoach route between Charleston and New Orleans." Present day Madisonians point out it is the "town Sherman refused to burn," although he did set fire to the depot.

Eatonton   *PUTNAM*   *1905*

Located on one of the largest public squares in the state, Putnam County's is one of the most beautiful courthouses. The original portion of this building was erected in 1824. Later remodeling featured more of the work of J. W. Golucke, including square brick columns supporting the two-story portico above the main entrance. An elaborate clock tower adds to the majestic splendor of the building. In 1905, W. J. Beeland contracted for an extensive remodeling of the building at a cost of $36,500. The cornerstone was laid on May 31, 1905 by the Grand Lodge F & AM of Georgia.

When the county was formed in 1807 from a portion of Baldwin County, it was named for General Israel Putnam, one of the heroes of the Battle of Bunker Hill. The county seat is named for William Eaton, a commander in the War with Tripoli in 1805.

The famous Rock Eagle Mound is located at the State 4-H Center. The county is also the home of Joel Chandler Harris, the creator of Uncle Remus.

Toccoa   *STEPHENS*   *1905*

Stephens County was created in 1905 from Franklin and Habersham counties. Built by the Falls Construction Company, the county's first and only courthouse is the design of M. T. Lewman, whose adaption of the traditional four column, two-story portico with clock tower blended form with function.

The county honors Alexander "Little Alex" Stephens, governor, senator and Vice-President of the Confederacy. Toccoa takes its name from the nearby falls of that name, which is the Cherokee word for "the beautiful." A typical early era fort and inn, once known as "Traveler's Rest," later called "Jarrett's Manor," is maintained as an historic site.

Sylvester　　　　　　　　**WORTH**　　　　　　　　*1905*

The first courthouse in Worth County burned in 1879. A schoolhouse was used until 1893 when a temporary courthouse was built. A more permanent structure was built in 1894 and it served until 1905 when it was replaced by another of J. W. Golucke's designs. The building featured columned portico entrances and a huge dome clock tower. Built by Totherow & Company, it cost $45,996.

On January 17, 1982, this historic old courthouse was destroyed by fire, despite the efforts of dozens of firemen from numerous communities throughout southwest Georgia. The fire, discovered at 2:45 a.m. caused the dome clock to crash through the roof, creating a draft that fanned the flames, overcoming the firemen's efforts. Fortunately, the records contained in the building had been microfilmed a few days earlier. It was reported that the fire was deliberately set by arsonists.

Worth County, once a part of Dooly and Irwin counties, is in one of the most fertile regions of the state. Created in 1853, it honors William J. Worth, a hero in the Mexican War and the son-in-law of General Zachary Taylor. The origin of the name of the county seat, Sylvester, has never been verified.

Newton **BAKER** *1906*

Baker County was created by the Legislature in 1825 from Early County. The county is named for Colonel John Baker, a hero of the Revolutionary War. The county seat is the namesake of Sergeant John Newton.

The original county seat was at Bryon, where the first courthouse was erected in 1826. Newton was named the county seat in 1831 and a wood courthouse was erected in 1832. The present brick courthouse was built in 1906 by Atlanta Fireproofing Company from plans by J. W. Golucke. Additions to the Clerk's vault and office were made in 1972. Baker County courthouses have been damaged or destroyed on three occasions by flood waters from the Flint River.

In 1836 the county was the scene of one of the fiercest battles of the Creek Indian War. It was in Baker that the Georgia Militia defeated a band of Indians, preventing the Creeks from joining the Seminoles in Florida.

Eastman   *DODGE*   *1906*

The creation of Dodge County in 1870 coincided with the advent of the lumber business in Georgia. The county seat is named for W. P. Eastman, an associate of William Dodge, for whom the county is named. Dodge, a New York industrialist, developer of the earliest mill towns in Georgia, congressman, and benefactor, presented Dodge County its first courthouse, a magnificent two-story frame building. In 1906, this frame structure was demolished and a two-story brick courthouse was erected for $125,000 by M. T. Lewman from the plans of architect E. C. Hosford.

Blakely *EARLY* *1906*

The flagstaff on the lawn of the Early County Courthouse at Blakely was the last to fly the Confederate flag in Georgia. Early is named for Peter Early, governor and U. S. senator. The county seat honors Captain Johnston Blakely, commander of the *USS WASP* during the War of 1812.

The county was created in 1818 from Indian lands and from it nine new counties were eventually constituted — Decatur, Seminole, Baker, Mitchell, Calhoun, Dougherty and parts of Clay, Grady, and Thomas.

From 1820 until 1825 court was held at the residence of Richard Grimsley in Blakely. In 1826 Benjamin Collier gave twenty-five acres to the county for the location of public buildings. Part of this tract includes the public square on which the present courthouse now stands.

Several small frame courthouses preceded a white pillared courthouse built in 1858. It was razed to make room for the present courthouse, which was completed in 1906 at a cost of $50,000. This two-and-one-half story building was built by W. T. Jay, a contractor from nearby Shellman. Designed by Morgan & Dillon, it features solid granite columns along the front colonnade and the traditional dome and clock tower.

Carnesville   **FRANKLIN**   *1906*

One of the oldest counties in the state, Franklin was the first county created after the Revolutionary War. Eleven Georgia and three South Carolina counties have been formed from Franklin.

Though organized in 1784, the first courthouse was not built until 1793. Prior to 1793 court was held at the home of Warren Philpot in the Gumlog District, and presided over by Judge George Walton, one of the signers of the Declaration of Independence. A second courthouse was built in 1826 and served until 1906 when the present courthouse was built at a cost of $44,797. W. Chamberlain & Company drew the plans for the neoclassic design which was built by M. T. Lewman. The pressed brick and concrete block were laid by a mason from New York who was paid $3.00 per day. He used a block and tackle which was pulled by a mule to hoist the bricks and the concrete. Arzo Dickson, a local resident, handled the mule by talking to him which attracted many sidewalk engineers of the day.

Franklin County honors Benjamin Franklin. The county seat is named for Judge Thomas Carnes. Franklin Springs was a popular summer resort in the 1800s.

Fitzgerald　　　　　　　　　　　　　*BEN HILL*　　　　　　　　　　　　　*1907*

Ben Hill County, carved from Irwin and Wilcox counties in 1906, is a tribute to Benjamin Harvey Hill, Georgia orator who served in the Georgia House and Senate, the Confederate Senate and in the U. S. Senate during Reconstruction.

The county seat is named for P. M. Fitzgerald, an Indiana editor who purchased and settled the surrounding 32,000 acres as a town for ex-Union soldiers immigrating from thirty eight states and two territories. The school they established was the first in Georgia to offer free textbooks and a nine-month school term.

The first courthouse, with some renovations, still serves Ben Hill County. The facility was erected in 1907 for $45,000 by the Falls City Construction Company of Kentucky from the design of Virginia architect H. H. Huggins. The style of the building resembles traditional neoclassicism with the stone colonades and clock tower (removed during 1954 renovations). Interior walls are plaster with marble wainscot and the floors, including the staircase to the courtroom, are marble. A portrait of Benjamin Harvey Hill hangs over the judges' bench.

Brunswick   *GLYNN*   *1907*

One of the original counties, Glynn was organized from the Anglican Parishes of St. David and St. Patrick in 1777. The county is named for John Glynn, a member of Parliament and staunch supporter of colonial rights.

The county is undisputed in its cultural, economic and political roles in the state. Recorded in the county courthouse are original land grants by King George II, including a grant to Button Gwinnett, a signer of the Declaration of Independence. It was in Glynn that General Oglethorpe ended Spanish colonial dreams in the Battle of Bloody Marsh in 1742, and the county is immortalized by Sidney Lanier in his "Marshes of Glynn."

Frederica served as the first county seat when Georgia's original constitution mandated "a Courthouse and gaol" to be built at local expense. In 1829, Brunswick was named the new county seat and court was held in the old Brunswick Bank & Trust Company, until a frame structure was built. This facility was replaced by a brick courthouse which was ravaged by a hurricane in 1896.

In 1907, the present two-story brick courthouse was erected. The building, with columned facades and surmounted by a cupola clock tower, is situated in the public square and is enveloped by colorful azaleas and huge moss-hung oak trees.

Mt. Vernon　　　　　　**MONTGOMERY**　　　　　*1907*

Montgomery County, created in 1794, has its roots in the period of Georgia's frontier. The first frame courthouse wasn't built in the original county seat of Smut until twenty years later because of the everpresent danger of Indian raids. The present courthouse was completed in 1907 at a cost of $36,480.

In 1859, the county seat was moved to its present location of Mount Vernon, which takes its name from the estate of George Washington. The county is named for General Richard Montgomery who was killed in the siege of Quebec in 1775.

The original county's boundaries included all of modern Tattnall and Wheeler counties and portions of Emanuel and Johnson counties. Today, Montgomery is one of the smallest counties in Georgia.

Ashburn   *TURNER*   *1907*

One of eight counties created in 1905, Turner still uses its original courthouse. This unique building boasts a freestanding steeple/clock tower rising from one corner of the structure, marble entrance floors, and brick masonry with stone accents.

The county name honors Henry Turner, congressman and justice of the Georgia Supreme Court. Ashburn, its county seat, is named for W. W. Ashburn, who instigated efforts to establish the area's lumber industry. The town has greater renown, however, as "The Peanut Capital of the World."

Baxley   *APPLING*   *1907-8*

Appling County was created from Indian lands obtained in the Creek Cession of 1814. On December 8, 1818 the Legislature provided that the first courthouse be built on land owned by Solomon Kennedy. The wooden frame structure was completed about 1830, and was destroyed by fire in the 1850s. The town of Holmesville grew up and prospered around the courthouse. The town gradually vanished after the county seat was moved to Baxley in 1874. Another wooden courthouse was built in Baxley and remained in service until 1907 when it was replaced by the present neoclassic structure. Designed by M. T. Lewman and built by Falls City Construction Company, the structure cost $20,000. In 1967 the courthouse underwent a major renovation, and an annex was added to house the jail and clerk of court.

At one time the original county included portions of Clinch, Telfair, Jeff Davis, Pierce, Ware, Charlton, Echols, Bacon and Wayne counties. Appling County is named for Colonel Daniel Appling who served in the War of 1812. Baxley was incorporated in 1875 and named for Wilson Baxley, an early settler of the area. Baxley is sometimes referred to as "The Turpentine Capital of the World." The Edwin I. Hatch Nuclear Power Plant, Georgia's first, began operation in Appling County in 1974.

Springfield   **EFFINGHAM**   *1908*

One of Georgia's original counties, Effingham was created in 1777 from the Anglican parishes of St. Matthew and St. Philip. Lord Effingham resigned his Royal commission in protest of British military action against the colonies, following the Declaration of Independence.

Springfield is the fifth seat of the county. The first two, Tucksee-king and Elberton, have since disappeared. The third, Ebenezer, was patterned after Savannah and served as the capital of Georgia for a brief period during the Revolutionary War. The town of Effingham laid claim to the seat from 1799 until the 1830s when Springfield became the permanent county seat.

Official records indicate that the earliest courthouse dates back to 1849. The present building, completed in 1908, features the Jeffersonian dome and cost about $40,000 to build.

Cairo   *GRADY*   *1908*

Grady County, named for Henry Grady, popular journalist, orator and advocate of the "New South," was created in 1905 from portions of Decatur and Thomas counties. The county seat, Cairo, derived its name from the Egyptian city located on the Nile River.

The courthouse was built three years later by J. B. Carr & Company from the design of Alexander Blair. The cost, $40,000, was paid in cash. The structure consisted of a traditional four-column facade with cupola clock tower. The outside was brick masonry on a stone foundation while the interior boasted plastered walls and wood paneling.

On February 19, 1980, this Grady County Courthouse was destroyed by fire.

Hamilton   *HARRIS*   *1908*

Harris County was named for Charles Harris, a prominent Savannah attorney and mayor while the county seat honors George W. Hamilton, a South Carolina statesman.

The county was constituted in 1827 from parts of Troup and Muscogee counties and has been served by three courthouses. A log courthouse served the area until it was replaced in 1831 by a more permanent structure. This facility continued in use until the present courthouse was completed in 1908. The courthouse features a distinctive six-column facade which is virtually the entire front of the building. The absence of a clock tower, included in many courthouses of the day, is particularly unusual. Other construction features include masonry bearing walls with wood floor framing and the slate pitched roof. The structure was built for $35,000 by the Mutual Construction Company, from plans by Ed. C. Hosford.

Harris County held its first election in 1828. It was the first county to adopt the County Commission form of government. It is the home of Callaway Gardens and the Franklin Delano Roosevelt State Park.

Monticello   *JASPER*   *1908*

In 1807 the county was organized as Randolph County and named for John Randolph of Virginia. Randolph fell into disrepute in Georgia because of his stand on various issues. In 1812, the General Assembly changed the name of the county to Jasper in honor of Sergeant William Jasper, the Revolutionary War hero killed in the siege of Savannah. Randolph gradually regained Georgian favor, and in 1828, the General Assembly named the present county of Randolph in his honor. Thus, he became the only person for whom two Georgia counties were named. The county seat, Monticello, is named for Thomas Jefferson's Virginia estate.

The first courthouse was a log cabin built in 1809 on a lot which was later sold to the county for fifty cents. Public business was first transacted in the home of John Towns. In 1907, the second courthouse was sold for seventy dollars with the stipulation that the purchaser remove the building and clear the site for use as a park. Upon removal, the building's cornerstone was found to contain a bottle of wine, various coins, copies of current newspapers and a list of county officials. The present courthouse was built in 1908, designed by the Lockwood Brothers with J.W. Beeland, contractor for the $44,400 project. The two-story building is Georgia marble and white brick with a four-column facade and an octagonal domed clock tower.

Thomaston   *UPSON*   *1908*

In 1824, Georgia required new counties with expanding settlements opening new lands in the west and the north. Upson County was created that year, and named for Stephen Upson, a member of the state legislature and trustee of the University of Georgia.

John Turner hosted the first session of Upson Superior Court in his home for fifty dollars rent The next year, 1828, saw the completion of the first courthouse for $10,000. Unfortunately, the structure was of such poor quality that the Grand Jury complained "the ten thousand dollar courthouse was being constructed of inferior lumber for the amount of money put into it." The building's walls began to crack in 1852 and the courthouse that replaced it lasted until the present building was completed in 1908 at a cost of $60,000.

Thomaston, the county seat, is the namesake of General Jett Thomas, a leader in the War of 1812. He would later attain another measure of fame by building the state capitol in Milledgeville.

Summerville   *CHATTOOGA*   *1909*

Named for the principal river flowing through the county, Chattooga was formed from parts of Floyd and Walker counties in 1838. The first courthouse, built in Summerville two years later, served until the present building was completed in 1909. The St. Louis architectural firm of Bryan & Associates designed the $60,000 structure which was built by the Falls City Construction Company of Louisville, Kentucky. Significant originality is displayed by a magnificent stained-glass window of the Great Seal of Georgia.

Chattooga contains the sites of several important Indian villages, Broom Town and Island Town, as well as Alpine, where Sequoyah, the inventor of the Indian alphabet, once resided. There are an endless number of stories as to how Summerville was named, but no agreement has been reached as to its derivation.

Warrenton　　　*WARREN*　　　*1909*

Warren County was carved from a portion of Wilkes in 1793. It was not until 1809 that a permanent courthouse was erected on the public square in Warrenton on land donated to the county by Dr. H. H. Tucker, an early chancellor of the University of Georgia. After a century of service, this courthouse was destroyed by fire. During that same year, 1909, the present courthouse was erected on the old site for $25,000. The building, designed by Walter Chamberlain, was built by Falls City Construction Company in the neoclassic style, with the four-columned facade adding imposing dignity.

Both the county and the county seat are named for General Joseph Warren, a hero of the Battle of Bunker Hill.

Ocilla　　　　　　　　*IRWIN*　　　　　　　　*1910*

The Irwin County courthouse, the fourth in Ocilla to lay such a claim, was completed in 1910 at a cost of $52,642. The first structure, built in 1839, was replaced fifteen years later. The third building was constructed in 1883 and lasted until the present courthouse began its tenure as the seat of county government. In 1972, substantial renovation added a modern finish to the brick masonry, updated the interior fixtures, and refinished both the cupola-type clock tower and the two four-columned facades.

Irwin County was named for Governor Jared Irwin, a Revolutionary War officer, and President of the Georgia Senate. The original county seat, also named for Irwin, gained notoriety as the site of Confederate President Jefferson Davis' capture by Union troops on May 10, 1865.

Millen   *JENKINS*   *1910*

In 1908, Jenkins County proudly opened its first courthouse, a beautiful colonial-style brick structure. Tragically, it burned to the ground in 1910. A. J. Franklin rebuilt the courthouse for $37,000 that same year, on the same site and identical to the first. L. F. Goodrich, the architect, is said to have reflected the "boundless optimism and pride of the early citizens" by including a sculpture on the clock tower of Blind Justice holding a lantern, but without her familiar scales.

The county is named for Charles J. Jenkins, Speaker of the Georgia House, Governor during Reconstruction, and President of the 1877 Georgia Constitutional Convention. Millen, the county seat, evolved from the number "seventy nine," the number of miles from Millen to Savannah.

An interesting historical note to the area around Millen involves Union soldiers during the Civil War. Sherman's men set fire to an old stagecoach stop in Birdsville and then quickly extinguished it when the mistress of the house refused to leave her sickbed.

Griffin *SPALDING* *1911*

Spalding County was established in 1851 from portions of Forsyth, Henry and Pike counties. Court sessions were held in the Griffin City Hall until 1859 when a large two-story brick building was erected. In 1910 the steeple and clock tower were removed from this building when it was converted into the county jail, a function it still serves. A modern courthouse, designed by A. Ten Eyck Brown, was completed in 1911 by the Newton Coal & Lumber Company. The four-columned building was destroyed by fire on January 12, 1981. While awaiting the completion of a new courthouse, a shopping center serves as a temporary court and county office building.

The county is the namesake of Colonel Thomas Spalding, a congressman and senator. The county seat is named in honor of General L. L. Griffin, the first president of the Monroe Railroad which later merged with the Central of Georgia.

The first Confederate monument erected in Georgia was unveiled in Spalding County in 1869. Spalding is also the location of the Agricultural Experiment Station.

Atlanta　　　　　　　　　*FULTON*　　　　　　　　*1912-14*

Fulton County was created from DeKalb County in 1853, with Atlanta the county seat. That same year, a courthouse/city hall was built on the present site of the State Capitol. The building served a double function as the State Capitol until 1884 when it was replaced by the present building. The second courthouse was built in 1884 at Pryor and Hunter streets. The present courthouse, Georgia's first million-dollar courthouse, was designed by A. Ten Eyck Brown and Morgan & Dillon Associates. At completion in 1914, the structure was one of the finest examples of beaux-arts classic architecture in the south. Campbell and Milton counties, consolidated with Fulton in 1932, prompted the establishment of regional courthouses in north and south Fulton County.

The county is named for the inventor of the steamboat, Robert Fulton. This fact which was officially established in 1954, was not specified in the original act creating the county, resulted in some speculation that the county was named for state engineer Hamilton Fulton. The county seat was originally named Terminus until 1842, when it was renamed Marthasville. In 1847 the city became Atlanta.

Tifton   *TIFT*   *1913*

Tift County sprung from portions of Berrien, Irwin, and Worth counties in 1905. The cornerstone of the courthouse was laid on December 12, 1912 in a Masonic ceremony. The columned structure remains, carefully carrying out its original function. The architect, W. A. Edwards, omitted the clock tower that adorns so many of Georgia's courthouses. The builder, J. F. Jenkins & Company, finished the job for $54,700.

The "Pathfinder of Southwest Georgia," Nelson Tift, is the man for whom the county and its seat are named. His nephew, H. H. Tift, was the founder of Tifton, having built a sawmill and commissary there in 1872.

The nationally known "Museum of Living Southern Agriculture," the Georgia Agrirama, attracts visitors to Tifton every year.

Cochran   *BLECKLEY*   *1914*

Bleckley County was developed from portions of Pulaski County in 1912. The county memorializes Logan Edwin Bleckley, one of the most distinguished Chief Justices of the Georgia Supreme Court. The county seat of Cochran, formerly known as Dykesboro, honors Judge Arthur E. Cochran, who was president of the old Macon and Brunswick Railroad.

The present courthouse, designed by Sayre &

Baldwin and built by Little & Cleckler Construction Company, was completed in 1914. During recent years, additions and renovations have been made to the stone-accented, brick masonry building.

Cochran, almost squarely in the center of the state, is the home of Middle Georgia College, established in 1927.

Athens   *CLARKE*   *1914*

Clarke County, best known as the home of the University of Georgia, is the namesake of Revolutionary War hero and frontiersman, Elijah Clarke. The confrontations during the 1870s between Athens and neighboring Watkinsville over the removal of the county seat, rival some of the more storied clashes on the gridiron at the University of Georgia for intensity. Watkinsville, the seat from the county's inception in 1801 until 1871, when it was moved to Athens, actually seceded from Clarke County over this uproar and eventually became the county seat of newly formed Oconee County. It is the only town to have been the county seat of two counties.

The courthouse in Athens is the third in the town. It was built in 1914 at a cost of $176,850, which was financed in part by a 4% bond. The unpainted brick edifice sits on a site graded by convict labor.

Winder   **BARROW**   *1915*

Barrow County was created in 1914 from parts of Gwinnett, Jackson, and Walton counties. The purpose for this new county was to alleviate the confusion in tax and business matters caused by the location of Winder at the juncture of these three counties. Barrow is named for David Crenshaw Barrow, chancellor of the University of Georgia for many years. The seat, known first as Jug Tavern, then Brandon, is named for General John H. Winder, noted railroad president.

The current courthouse was built in 1915 by the R. W. Wimbish Company from the plans of J. J. Baldwin. Most notable features include concrete floors, exterior brick walls, interior marble wainscoting with wood panels.

At nearby Fort Yargo a log blockhouse was built in 1793 to protect early settlers from the Indians, and the site is now a state park. Barrow County is also home of the Russell family, one of Georgia's most prominent in both state and national politics.

Preston   **WEBSTER**   *1915*

In 1861, the first Confederate flag to fly in Georgia was raised on the Webster County Courthouse lawn, where the first courthouse in the county is remembered for its demise. Built in 1860, the building was destroyed by fire in 1914. It was reported that "In September 1914 an investigation started concerning the disposition of certain court funds. Things got pretty hot. Around 10:45 PM, Sunday, September 27th, the courthouse was discovered to be on fire. The first upon the scene stated that a fire was burning at the foot of the stairs and the odor of kerosene filled the air. County records were almost a total loss. . . . Arson was probably the cause of the fire but no one was ever arrested for the crime."

The second and current courthouse was erected a year later by Shields, Geise & Rawlings from a design by T. F. Lockwood, Sr. The most notable feature is the belvedere instead of the traditional clock tower.

Webster County was carved from Randolph in 1853. The original name of the county, Kinchafoonee, an Indian name, drew state-wide derision and laughter, resulting in the change in 1856 to honor the American statesman Daniel Webster. At the same time the county seat, McIntosh, was changed to Preston, in honor of William O. Preston.

Lincolnton　　　　　**LINCOLN**　　　　　*1916*

Lincoln County was established in 1796 from Wilkes County. The county and county seat are named for Major General Benjamin Lincoln, designated by General Washington to accept Lord Cornwallis' sword at the surrender of Yorktown. Lincoln later served as Secretary of War under President Washington. Of the thirteen United States "Lincoln Counties," Georgia's is the only one not named for the sixteenth President.

Prior to the adoption in 1800 of Lincolnton as the county seat, the first court cases were held at the home of Josiah Stovall. With the move to Lincolnton came Lincoln County's first courthouse, a square-rock building. The second courthouse, an oblong, two-story hipped roof structure, was built in 1874 in the public square and continued to be used until 1916.

In 1916 the third and current, courthouse was erected at a cost of $30,000 by the Little & Cleckler Construction Company from a design of architect Lloyd Preacher. The exterior of the building is dominated by stately columns and magnificent porticos, crowned by a clock tower with four dials. Surrounding landscaping and additions to this facility are in keeping with the original style.

Chatsworth   *MURRAY*   *1916*

Established in 1832, Murray County commemorates Thomas Walton Murray, Speaker of the Georgia House, who was living when the honor was bestowed, a rare tribute to his legislative accomplishments.

The first county seat was Spring Place, known for its spring water and as a natural meeting place for Cherokees and early settlers. The two-story brick courthouse was converted into a schoolhouse when the seat of government moved to Chatsworth in 1912.

Alexander Blair designed the courthouse for the new county seat, blending a Jeffersonian dome with Palladian styling in the circa-1916 structure.

Alamo   *WHEELER*   *1917*

Wheeler County, formed from a part of Montgomery in 1912, honors Confederate Cavalry leader General "Joe" Wheeler. He served as Federal Cavalry Commander during the Spanish-American War at the Battle of Santiago, made famous by the Teddy Roosevelt Rough Riders' charge up San Juan Hill. The seat, Alamo, commemorates the site in Texas where Americans fought to the last man for Texas independence.

The first courthouse in Wheeler County was short-lived, built in 1914 and destroyed by fire in 1916. The E. C. Hosford Company erected the present structure in 1917 with its most notable features the columned facades on all four sides. The red brick building was completely renovated in 1961.

Gibson   *GLASCOCK*   *1918*

Glascock County, one of the smallest in size and population, was created in 1857 from Warren County. It was named for General Thomas Glascock, a veteran of the War of 1812 and the Seminole War. He later served in the Georgia Legislature and in Congress. In 1858, Judge William Gibson donated $500 toward the building of the first courthouse, with the county seat being named for him.

In 1918, the two-story frame courthouse was moved from its original site, where it is now the Kent family residence. Its replacement, of brick masonry with stone accents, was designed and built by J. W. McMillian & Sons.

Leesburg   *LEE*   *1918*

The first record of a courthouse is of one built at Starkville in 1837. Another courthouse erected in 1854 was destroyed by fire two years later. A brick courthouse was built in Leesburg in 1861, only to suffer the same fate as its predecessor. The present structure was built in 1918, at a cost of $40,000. The exterior exhibits brick masonry with stone accents, columned facades and a simple clock tower. The interior is noted for the terrazzo tiled floors.

Lee County, an original county created from the Creek Cessions of 1826, has had two county seats in its existence. The first, Starkville, was the site of two courthouses while Leesburg, originally named Wooten Station, has been the location for three facilities. The county and the county seat are named for Colonel Richard Henry "Lighthorse Harry" Lee, father of Confederate General Robert E. Lee.

Alma   *BACON*   *1919*

The county was named for one of Georgia's outstanding United States Senators, Augustus Octavius Bacon of Macon who died at the age of eighty-six in 1914, the year the county was created. The county seat derives its name from the first letter of Georgia's capitals — Augusta, Louisville, Milledgeville, and Atlanta. Bacon County, one of the youngest counties, was created from Appling, Pierce, and Ware counties.

The only courthouse was completed in 1919 by R. W. Wimbish, with J. J. Baldwin as architect. It is a handsome structure built on the "Y" design, facing the corner of the public square, and crowned with a clock tower. The exterior walls are unpainted face brick with wood cornice. Interior walls are a combination of plaster and wood paneling.

Lafayette   **WALKER**   *1919*

Created from Murray County in 1833, Walker is named for Freeman Walker, member of the Georgia House and U. S. Senate, who served as the first mayor of Augusta. The county seat, Lafayette, originally Chattooga, honors the Marquis de La Fayette.

The county was the site of one of the bloodiest battles in the War Between the States. At Chickamauga Creek in 1863, the most vicious battle ever fought in Georgia claimed more than 28,000 casualties. The battlefield was the first to be set aside as a National Battlefield Park by the Department of the Interior.

Walker has had four courthouses, the first a structure built by the Cherokee Indians thirteen years before creation of the county. A second building, erected in 1838, was destroyed by fire in 1883 and replaced by a third building which was in service until 1919, when the present beaux-arts Rennaissance Revival courthouse was completed. Built by Little & Cleckler Construction Company for $100,000, the bond-financed project features rounded brick masonry columns with Georgia marble trim. The architect, C. E. Beardon, designed a facility of rare style in Southern public buildings.

Pearson   *ATKINSON*   *1920*

One of the youngest counties, Atkinson was created from portions of Coffee and Clinch counties in August, 1917. It honors William Y. Atkinson, a native of Coweta County, who served as Governor of Georgia from 1894 to 1898. The county seat takes its name from a family of early settlers in the county.

The first — and present — courthouse, designed by J. J. Baldwin and built by Holly Construction Company, was completed in 1920. It is a three-story red brick structure with limestone trim. The interior walls are painted plaster and wood paneling. The building was recently remodeled to include windows and doors using combinations of wood, aluminum and glass.

Soperton   *TREUTLEN*   *1920*

Created in 1917, Treutlen County is one of Georgia's youngest counties. It is named for John Adam Treutlen, the first governor of Georgia following statehood. Treutlen, believed to have been killed by Tories, was known as "one of the foremost revolutionists," when he defeated Button Gwinnett for governor in 1777. The county seat is named for Mr. Soper, a prominent citizen of the time.

Treutlen's only courthouse was erected in 1920 for $75,000 by the I. P. Crutchfield Construction Company from a design by J. J. Baldwin. The decor is traditional with face brick and limestone, columned portico and clock tower. Last renovations to the building were made in 1976.

1920 to 1945

Metter   *CANDLER*   *1921*

After a ten year "battle" in the Legislature, Candler County was finally created in 1914 from portions of Bulloch, Emanuel, and Tattnall counties. It is named for Allen D. Candler, a Governor of Georgia and prominent compiler of Revolutionary and Confederate records of the state. Due to an eye injury he sustained during the War Between the States, he was known as the "one-eyed plowboy from Pigeon Roost."

The well-kept courthouse was designed by J. J. Baldwin and built by King Lumber Company for $125,000. The exterior walls are brick with stone accents.

Candler County is located on the old Sunbury Road which connected the early seaport of Sunbury in Liberty County with the upland plantations.

Donalsonville   *SEMINOLE*   *1921*

Seminole County is one of four counties in Georgia named for Indian tribes. It was created in 1920 from portions of Decatur and Early counties. The county seat, incorporated in 1897, honors Jonathan E. Donalson, a prominent local resident. Within the county is the historic "Three Notch Trail," an obscure Indian route that General Andrew Jackson followed and blazed with three notches during the Seminole War.

Seminole County's present courthouse is the only one it has had. The beaux-arts classic structure was designed and built by William J. J. Chase for $85,000, a price which included construction of the jail. Although maintaining the traditional four-column, two-story portico over the main entrance, the steeple was eliminated, leaving the tower just large enough to enclose the clock. The courthouse grounds are one of the few in Georgia landscaped with palm trees.

Claxton   *EVANS*   *1923*

The Evans County Courthouse is one of the most beautiful designs of J. J. Baldwin. The only courthouse that Evans County has had, it is noted for the lighted clock in the dome topping the four-columned portico which extends the full height of the two-story building. The structure was built by West Point Construction Company for $60,000 on land donated by Terrell Trapwell, one of the founders of the city of Metter.

The county is named for General Clement A. Evans who commanded the Confederate division which made the last charge at Appomattox. Claxton, formerly called Hendrix, is known as the "Fruitcake Capital of the World."

Lumpkin   *STEWART*   *1923*

The present courthouse is Stewart County's fifth. The first courthouse was a log cabin erected in 1831, a year after the county was created from Randolph County. A more substantial building was completed in 1837 and served until a brick structure replaced it in 1895. In 1923 a fire nearly destroyed it. Rebuilt by T. F. Lockwood, Jr., it features an unusual location of the clock tower. Using inmate labor, the building was renovated in 1983.

The county is named for General Daniel Stewart who fought in both the Revolutionary War and the War of 1812. He was also the maternal grandfather of Theodore Roosevelt. The county seat is named for Wilson Lumpkin, governor and prominent leader in early Georgia politics.

Providence Canyon, created by erosion over the past seventy years, is a national tourist attraction as is "Westville," a recreated Georgia town where "it is always 1850." The county is a beautiful landscape of rolling hills paralleling Lake Walter George.

Macon   *BIBB*   *1924*

Created in 1822, Bibb County has had four courthouses. The first was a one-room building, erected in 1825 at the corner of Mulberry and Third streets. The second courthouse was built in 1828 for $12,750. The three-story brick structure was for many years considered one of the finest courthouses in the state. A more spacious three-story courthouse was constructed in 1870 at a cost of $100,000. Located at Second and Mulberry streets, it was built of brick and crowned with a clock tower.

The present courthouse, completed in 1924, was designed by Curran R. Ellis. The lobby area floors are marble. In 1926 a jail was added to the top floor and in 1940 the building underwent extensive remodeling as a WPA project.

Bibb County is named for an early Georgia doctor, William Wyatt Bibb, who also served in the U. S. Senate and as the first territorial governor of Alabama. The county seat honors Nathaniel Macon of North Carolina. Macon is the home of Wesleyan College, the first in the world to award degrees to women. Mercer University was relocated in Macon in 1871. Adjacent to the city are the famous Ocmulgee Indian Mounds.

Irwinton   *WILKINSON*   *1924*

Wilkinson County is one of three created from the Creek Cessions of 1803-06. It honors General James Wilkinson, a hero of the Revolutionary War while the county seat is named for Governor Jared Irwin.

The first Superior Court was held near Irwinton, but it wasn't until 1829 that a courthouse was built and lost to fire in the same year. Its replacement was also destroyed by fire. A fourth, more substantial courthouse was built and remained in service until it was replaced in 1924 by the present brick structure.

This area of Georgia provided some of the fiercest resistance to Sherman's "bummers" and local pride is bolstered by the report of a one-legged Confederate who single-handedly held off the federal troops for four hours at Gordon.

Wilkinson County is rich in kaolin mineral deposits, one of Georgia's most important natural resources.

Canton   *CHEROKEE*   *1926*

Cherokee County was created on December 26, 1831, from lands ceded by the Cherokee Indians and the name honors them. Originally covering most of north Georgia, twenty two counties were carved from Cherokee. Although the origin of the name of the county seat is not documented, it probably got its name from Canton, the Chinese silk center, as a tribute to the early Georgians who tried in vain to establish a silk industry in the Colony.

Court was first held in a log cabin near the house of John Lay on Cumming Street. A second courthouse was burned by Sherman's raiders in 1864. For the following nine years court was held in the old Presbyterian Church. A red brick courthouse was built in 1874 at a cost of $10,000. It was destroyed by fire in 1928. The present courthouse, built of white marble, is considered one of the finest public buildings in Georgia. Designed by A. Ten Eyck Brown, it was constructed by J. S. McCauley in 1928 for $149,036.59.

Trenton   *DADE*   *1926*

Dade County, constituted on December 25, 1837, has often been called the Legislature's "Christmas present to the State." It is named in honor of Major Francis Dade who had been killed two years earlier by the Indians in the Florida campaign. The county seat takes its name from the Battle of Trenton when Washington surprised the Hessians celebrating Christmas.

The first courthouse was built in 1849 and is generally believed to have been burned by Sherman in 1864, although the county had seceded from Georgia at the outbreak of the War Between the States.

A second courthouse was destroyed by fire in 1895. The present courthouse, a modified federal design, was built by the Barrett Construction Company for $31,000 in 1926.

Hinesville   *LIBERTY*   *1926*

Liberty, the first of four counties in the nation to be so named, was created from the Anglican parishes of St. John, St. Andrew, and St. James in 1777. It commemorates the patriotism of the uncompromising champions of freedom, the settlers at Midway and Sunbury, many of whom had emigrated from New England. Sunbury, a principal colonial seaport, has vanished. Two members of the Midway Church, one of the state's most cherished shrines, were Dr. Lyman Hall and Button Gwinnett, both signers of the Declaration of Independence. The county seat is named for the Hines family, early settlers of the region.

The first record of a courthouse indicates it was a small wooden structure built in 1849. It was replaced in 1867 and that courthouse served until the present one, designed by J. J. Baldwin, was built in 1926. Two wings were added in 1964, reflecting the county's growth in recent years.

Ludowici   *LONG*   *1926*

With the establishment of nationwide "standard time," the courthouse clock became more traditional than functional. The Long County Courthouse, built in 1926, is typical of the design of the early twentieth century — columned portico, brick with limestone trim, but no clock tower.

A marker on the courthouse grounds reads: "This county is named for Dr. Crawford Long, who first used ether as an anesthetic in a surgical operation at Jefferson, Georgia on March 30, 1842. Born in Danielsville, November 1, 1815, Dr. Long was a graduate of Franklin College (now the University of Georgia)."

The county seat is named for German tile manufacturer Carl Ludowici, who settled in the area.

Woodbine **CAMDEN** *1928*

Camden, Georgia's southernmost county, was created by the Constitution of 1777 and is named for Charles Pratt, Earl of Camden, Lord Chancellor of England who strongly advocated home rule for the colonies.

The first frame courthouse was built in the early 1800s at Jefferson, later known as Jeffersonton. In 1871 the county seat was relocated at St. Patrick, later named St. Marys. In 1923, the county seat was moved to Woodbine, about six miles from Jefferson, which has since vanished from the map.

The present courthouse, a twentieth-century Gothic Revival, is the only one of its style in Georgia. It was designed by J. DeBruyn Kops and was built by the McCowan & Ramsey Company for $59,000.

The first domestic pecans were grown at St. Marys from nuts found floating in the sea. With the news of the death of George Washington, the townsfolk held a formal funeral procession with a flag-draped coffin for burial near one of the town wells. Four liveoak trees were planted at the site, one of which still survives.

Carrollton   *CARROLL*   *1928*

Carroll, created from the Creek Indian Cessions in 1825, was once known as the "Free State of Carroll" because of its huge size. It honors Charles Carroll, who died at the age of ninety five — the last survivor of the fifty six signers of the Declaration of Independence. At his funeral the Liberty Bell was tolled for the last time. The county seat commemorates Carroll's Maryland estate.

The first record of a courthouse dates back to 1849, twenty years after Carrollton was moved to its present location. In the 1880s a brick courthouse was erected on the public square and served until 1927, when it burned. The present courthouse, completed in 1928, was designed by William J. J. Chase and built by Carr Construction Company for $166,983. The foundation is reinforced concrete with stone facing and cornices. The 3200-square-foot courtroom with its twenty-five foot ceiling is the largest in the state.

Carroll County was the scene of Georgia's first gold discovery in 1826, three years before the big gold rush near Dahlonega.

Folkston   *CHARLTON*   *1928*

When the county was created in 1854, Trader's Hill was selected as the county seat. The first courthouse, a two-story wooden building was constructed immediately. It was destroyed by fire in 1877, resulting in a loss of most of the county records. The county seat was moved to Folkston in 1901 and a courthouse was built there in 1902. It was destroyed by fire in 1928. The present courthouse was designed by Roy A. Benjamin in the Georgian Revival style. It was built by Basil P. Kennard for $54,476.29, with the clock tower costing an additional $3,091.61.

Charlton County is named for Robert M. Charlton of Savannah who served in the U.S. Senate and as regent of the Smithsonian Institution. He died the year the county was created. The county seat is named for the Folks family, prominent local citizens of the area.

A large portion of the county lies within the Okefenokee Swamp, a 400,000-acre wildlife sanctuary, one of the nation's largest.

Nahunta   *BRANTLEY*   *1930*

The first courthouse in Brantley County was built in Hoboken in 1921. The present courthouse was built in Nahunta in 1930. The two-story brick structure, which cost $29,286, has interior walls of painted plaster with wood wainscoting. In 1978 additions and renovations cost $234,000.

Created in 1921 from Charlton, Pierce, and Wayne counties, Brantley is one of the youngest in the state. The name honors State Senator Benjamin D. Brantley. Originally called Victoria, Nahunta is often mistaken for an Indian name. It actually derives its origin from railroad maps and a sign "N. A. Hunter Siding." Mr. N. A. Hunter was an early settler and railroad customer.

Barnesville   *LAMAR*   *1931*

Lamar County's only courthouse was formally opened on October 19, 1931. Neoclassic in design, Eugene C. Wachendorff was the architect and the Barnesville Planing Mill Company the builder.

The county was organized in 1920, making it the second youngest of Georgia's counties. For the first ten years office space was rented and the Masonic Building on Main Street was used for the semiannual sessions of Superior Court and sessions of the County Court.

Lamar County is the offspring of Monroe and Pike counties and is named for the famed Lucius Quintus Cincinnatus Lamar, congressman, cabinet secretary under Cleveland, and a Justice of the U.S. Supreme Court.

The county seat is the namesake of Gideon Barnes, who established a tavern and stagecoach stop in 1820 on the old Alabama Road. Barnesville was once the hub of buggy building in the state.

Ellijay　　　　　　　　　*GILMER*　　　　　　　　　*1934*

The first courthouse in Gilmer County was a small wooden structure erected in 1833. Another courthouse was built in 1854 but by the 1930s the space had become inadequate. In 1934 an old hotel on the public square was converted into a courthouse and it is still in use today. At one time known as the Hyatt Hotel, it was built in 1898. It is the only multi-storied courthouse now in use with the courtroom on the first floor.

Gilmer County was created in 1832 and named for George R. Gilmer, one of Georgia's early governors, congressman, veteran of the Creek War, and regent of the University of Georgia. The county seat, often called the "Apple Capital of Georgia," takes its name from "Ellija," an old Indian village.

McRae   *TELFAIR*   *1934*

A frame courthouse was built at Jacksonville in 1852, after Telfair County was created from Wilkinson in 1807. A brick structure, built in 1807 when the county seat was relocated at McRae, was destroyed by fire.

The present building, designed by the Macon architects Dennis & Dennis, is unique in that the colonaded facade supports the portico above the main entrance. A. E. Ittner of Albany was the contractor for the 1934 project.

The county honors Edward Telfair, member of the Continental Congress who later served as governor. McRae is named for a Scotch family who were early settlers in the area. It is also well known as the home of Governor Eugene Talmadge, the "Sage of Sugar Creek."

Morgan   *CALHOUN*   1935

The selection of a seat for a newly created county was often a touchy, if not highly controversial, subject. When Calhoun County was constituted in 1854 from Baker and Early, prominent families in Concord and Whitney compromised by locating the county seat exactly halfway between the communities. A handkerchief was tied to the wheel of a buggy and the revolutions counted on the route between the two settlements. They then drove back half the number of turns of the wheel and built the courthouse on that site. The town of Morgan grew up around the courthouse. The first Superior Court was held there on December 18, 1854.

There have been three courthouses, all built on the same site. The first one was destroyed by fire in 1888. A new courthouse was built and it also was destroyed by fire. The present courthouse was built in 1935 for $30,000 by T. F. Lockwood, Jr. It was renovated in 1972.

Calhoun County is named for Senator John C. Calhoun of South Carolina. The county seat was first named Jasper but was later changed to honor General Daniel Morgan, although there is local dispute over the validity of this claim.

Butler   *TAYLOR*   *1935*

A beautiful two-story brick courthouse was erected in Taylor County shortly after it was organized in 1852. It was torn down in 1935 to make way for the present courthouse. Built by M. Entrekin Company from plans by F. Roy Duncan, it follows the traditional style with a white columned portico, although the cupola and clock tower are rather small.

Taylor County was created from Macon, Marion, and Talbot counties and honors Zachary Taylor, a hero of the Mexican War and President of the United States. The county seat is the namesake of William Orlando Butler, poet and Mexican War general.

Fort Valley   PEACH   *1936*

Peach is the youngest county in Georgia, created by the General Assembly on July 18, 1924 from Houston and Macon counties. The only courthouse to serve the county was erected in 1936 by the Griffin Construction Company from plans by Dennis & Dennis. In deference to custom, a small cupola was placed on top but it does not have a clock.

The county honors the most prominent fruit of Georgia — the peach. The county seat, incorporated in 1836 as Fox Valley, was "misread" in the Legislative act. Residents felt it was easier to change the name of the town than to have the enactment rewritten. Fort Valley is the home of Fort Valley State College.

Blue Ridge   *FANNIN*   *1937*

The first courthouse in Fannin, a small wooden structure built at Morgantown, was destroyed by fire. In 1895 the county seat was moved to Blue Ridge, named for the beautiful southern reach of the Appalachian Mountains. A brick two-story structure was built and it was destroyed by fire in 1936. The present courthouse was built a year later by Beers & Collins from the plans of Edwards, Sayward & Robert B. Logan Associates.

The county was created in 1854 from Gilmer and Union counties. It memorializes Colonel James W. Fannin, the leader of a band of 500 soldiers who were killed by the Mexicans at Goliad Massacre.

Mitchell County has had four courthouses since it was organized in 1857. The first, a two-story wooden structure built in 1858, met the fate of many wooden courthouses when it was destroyed by fire in 1869. The following year an exact duplicate was built on the same location. It served until 1890 when a more spacious courthouse was built. After almost fifty years of service, it was replaced in 1937 by the present imposing structure.

According to *Knight's Legends,* the county is named for General David Mitchell, a native of Scotland who served two terms as Governor of Georgia. Camilla, the county seat, honors his daughter. Another claim has the county named for General Henry Mitchell of the Georgia Militia, and President of the Georgia Senate.

The city of Pelham is a county tribute to Major John Pelham who, while still a teenager, was commander of Jeb Stuart's horse artillery during the War Between the States.

Pembroke   *BRYAN*   *1938*

Bryan County, created in 1793 from Chatham County, is named for a member of the King's Council, Johnathan Bryan, who accompanied Oglethorpe to the Colony, and later joined the fight against British rule.

Hardwicke, laid out in 1755, was the temporary county seat but no courthouse was ever erected there. No longer in existence, it was once suggested as Georgia's capital.

An Act of 1797 designated the county seat as Cross Roads, two miles from the Ogeechee bridge. A wooden courthouse was built in 1854 and the site became known as Bryan Courthouse. In 1860 Eden was named the county seat and a frame courthouse was built. In 1901 a two-story courthouse was built at Clyde, and it served until the area was cleared for the construction of Fort Stewart.

Pembroke became the county seat and the present courthouse was built in 1938. An annex was added in 1969. The courthouse is considered one of the most picturesque sites in the Coastal Plains, sometimes called the "pine barrens."

Ringgold   *CATOOSA*   *1939*

Catoosa County was created from parts of Walker and Whitfield counties in 1853. Some sources say that it is named for an Indian chief, others for Catoosa Springs, just east of Ringgold. The county seat honors Major Samuel Ringgold of Maryland who was killed in the first battle of the Mexican War.

The original courthouse was a two-story 60' x 40' structure built in 1856 for $6,845 on land donated by W. B. W. Dent. Permission was given the Masons to build a third floor to use as a Masonic Hall. This third floor is credited with saving county records, as Sherman ordered the fire started by his men extinguished when he arrived and saw that the Masonic Lodge was housed in the courthouse.

The present courthouse was built in 1939 as a PWA project. Crutchfield & Law were the architects and Barrett Construction Company the contractors.

In the Battle of Ringgold the stone depot was in the center of some of the fiercest fighting. It was rebuilt and is now Georgia's oldest railroad depot still in service.

Adel   *COOK*   *1939*

Cook, one of Georgia's newer counties, was created by an Act of July 30, 1918. It was formed from Berrien County.

The second floor of the City Hall in Adel served as the first courthouse for the county. A second building, a two-story garage, was used as a courthouse until the present courthouse was built in 1939. It is a two-story brick structure on a concrete foundation.

The county is named in honor of Congressman and Georgia Secretary of State Philip Cook who gained fame as the leader of the Doles-Cook Brigade in the War Between the States. It is not generally known how Adel, the county seat, got its name. Just east of Adel are the Lime Sinks, a series of lakes which residents say are bottomless.

Watkinsville　　　　　　　　　　　　*OCONEE*　　　　　　　　　　　　*1939*

Watkinsville was the county seat of Clarke County until 1871, when Athens replaced it. The residents of Watkinsville were so incensed they secured the creation of Oconee County, and Watkinsville once again became a county seat.

The first courthouse was built at Watkinsville in 1806 and another in 1849. A new courthouse was erected in 1875 when Oconee was created. The present modern brick building was completed in 1939 and has subsequently been renovated.

Oconee County is named for the river which forms its eastern boundary. The county seat honors Augusta lawyer Robert Watkins. The Eagle Tavern in Watkinsville is said to be one of the reasons for the choice of Athens over Watkinsville for the site of the University of Georgia.

Georgetown   *QUITMAN*   *1939*

Quitman County, created in 1858, has had only two courthouses. The first was a two-story wooden structure erected soon after the county was organized. It burned in 1920 and a rented warehouse served as a courthouse until 1939. At that time the present attractive brick courthouse was built. It was designed by T. F. Lockwood, Jr. and built by D. M. Still. The building adequately serves the needs of the county, which is one of the least populous and smallest counties in the state.

Quitman, carved from Randolph and Stewart counties in 1858, is named for Mexican War hero and Governor of Mississippi, John A. Quitman. Georgetown is named for its District of Columbia counterpart. Much of the original county was inundated with the formation of Lake Walter George on the Chatta-hoochee River.

Conyers　　　　　　　　　　*ROCKDALE*　　　　　　　　　　*1939*

Rockdale County, named for the belt of granite underlying the region, built its first courthouse soon after it was created from Henry and Newton in 1870. The Williamsburg-style courthouse was built in 1939 and the tremendous growth of the region necessitated an additional three-story brick facility for the court and the county offices.

The county seat is named for Dr. Conyers, a noted advocate of temperance. The Cistercian Monastery, built by the monks, is a tourist attraction of the county.

LaGrange   *TROUP*   *1939*

Troup County, formed in 1826 from the Creek Cessions is named for Governor George M. Troup, the "Hercules of States' Rights." He is one of the few honored by having a county named for him while still living.

The first session of Troup Superior Court was held in 1827 at a private home near LaGrange. In 1828 LaGrange, named for the ancestral home of the Marquis de La Fayette, was selected as the county seat. Two years later a brick courthouse was erected. This building was later supplemented with two small offices, separated by a vault, for the clerk and ordinary. The old brick courthouse and offices were dismantled in 1904, when the second courthouse was built, which burned in 1936.

The present courthouse was built of Tennessee marble and completed in 1939. Designed by William J. J. Chase, it was built by the A. J. Hunnicut Company. The public square was converted to a park which features a statue of La Fayette atop a colored-light fountain.

Douglas   *COFFEE*   *1940*

The first Coffee County courthouse, built shortly after the county was created in 1854 from Clinch, Irwin, Telfair, and Ware, was lost in a fire in 1898. The second courthouse, built in 1902, was a victim of fire in 1930. The present courthouse, completed in 1940, is brick with limestone accents.

The county is the namesake of John Coffee, Georgia Militia General in the Creek War, who later served as state senator and congressman. The county seat memorializes Stephen A. Douglas of Illinois, famed for his debates with Abraham Lincoln.

Swainsboro   *EMANUEL*   *1940*

Emanuel County was created from Bulloch and Montgomery counties in 1812 and is named for David Emanuel, Revolutionary War soldier who was one of Georgia's early governors.

The history of Emanuel County courthouses is typical of the period — the first, built in 1814, burned in 1841; the second, completed in 1845, was a victim of fire in 1857. Three other courthouses of varying size were built and subsequently abandoned until the present marble structure was completed in 1940.

In 1814 the county seat was designated as one mile from the center of the county. In 1822 it was named Swainsboro for a local family. In 1854 the name was changed to Paris but the original name was soon revived.

1945 to 1983

Jasper   *PICKENS*   *1949*

With Judge David Irwin presiding, the first session of the Superior Court of Pickens County was held "under spacious oak" on May 15, 1854, soon after the county was created from Cherokee and Gilmer counties in 1853. The first courthouse, a handsome brick structure, was completed in 1859. The second courthouse, a two-story brick building with a columned portico over the main floor entrance, was destroyed by fire in 1947.

Marble is the leading product of the county and the present courthouse, completed in 1949, is marble over masonry construction.

Pickens County was named for General Andrew Pickens, and the county seat for Sergeant William Jasper, both heroes of the Revolution. According to reports, since Pickens County never seceded from the Union, the United States' flag flew above the courthouse during the War Between the States.

Cordele   *CRISP*   *1950*

Crisp County is named for Charles Frederick Crisp of Americus, Congressman and Speaker of the U. S. House of Representatives. Cordele, founded in 1888 as a railroad junction, honors Cordelia Hawkins, daughter of the president of the Savannah, Americus, and Montgomery Railroad.

The first courthouse in Crisp County was a handsome two-story brick structure built in 1907. It was destroyed by fire in 1950, but most of the valuable records were saved. The second and present courthouse was erected in 1950 at a cost of $223,425 by S. J. Curry & Company. It is a modern design by Bernard A. Webb, Jr., with brick veneer over concrete masonry. One man was killed in 1982 when a homemade bomb designed to destroy the courthouse exploded prematurely a few feet from the building; his partner was later convicted for felony murder. The two men were allegedly hired to bomb the courthouse to destroy records in a drug case.

Crisp County is the first county in the nation to own and operate an electrical power plant.

Perry   *HOUSTON*   *1950*

This courthouse reflects the growing prosperity and development of Houston County. The building was designed by E. Oren Smith and constructed by S. J. Curry & Company of brick veneer over block cavity wall with a concrete foundation. It was completed in 1950 at a cost of $325,000.

Houston County is the namesake of the famed patriot, Governor John Houston. The county seat, Perry, honors Naval Captain Oliver H. Perry who defeated the British in the Battle of Lake Erie.

Warner Robins, the largest city in the county, is the home of Robins Air Force Base, and the site of a "satellite" courthouse, the first of its kind in Georgia.

Cedartown   *POLK*   *1951*

Polk County's present courthouse, completed in 1951, is a modern building designed by William J. J. Chase. Built by Bailey-Brazzel Construction Company, its brick masonry and limestone construction is more functional than decorative. The first courthouse, erected in 1852, was destroyed by fire in 1856. The second courthouse was not completed until 1867. The third courthouse, completed in 1891, was a conventional red brick building with a steeple and clock tower. It served the county until 1951, when the present courthouse was built.

Polk County, created from Floyd and Paulding counties in 1851, honors President James K. Polk. Cedartown, the county seat, was originally the site of a Cherokee Indian village, and is fittingly named for the cedar trees which flourish in this beautiful valley.

Statenville   *ECHOLS*   *1956*

The county seat of Statenville, though spelled Statesville in the enabling act, is unique in that it has zero population. Its population in 1958 was about five hundred when a bill was passed by the General Assembly restricting the city limits to the courthouse block, excluding all residents. Thus, all Statenville residents are residents of the county only.

Founded in 1858, the county is named for Robert M. Echols, a member of the General Assembly, who served as a Brigadier General in the Mexican War.

The first Echols County courthouse was a frame building erected in 1859. In the late 1870s, a new, two-story wooden building was erected which was destroyed by fire in 1897; all records were lost, except for two deed books. Pending the erection of another courthouse, the Grand Jury used the Masonic Hall for its meetings, and court was held in a local church.

In 1898 the commissioners rented a storehouse for $1.50 per month for use as a temporary courthouse. On September 15, 1899, the county accepted a new two-story wooden structure from the contractor. A vault was added in 1908. The present brick courthouse was built in 1956 by Elza D. Smith Construction Company.

Douglasville   **DOUGLAS**   *1957*

The first courthouse in Douglas County was a wooden structure built in 1874; the second, built of brick, was destroyed by fire. The present modern courthouse was built in 1957.

Douglas County was carved from Campbell and Carroll counties in 1870. Both the county and the county seat are named for the "Little Giant," Stephen A. Douglas, a U. S. Senator and candidate for President in 1860. Herschel V. Johnson of Georgia was his running mate. The ticket lost to Abraham Lincoln.

Douglasville was originally known as Skinned Chestnut because the Indians stripped bark from a chestnut tree to better mark it as a meeting place.

Waycross   *WARE*   *1957*

The first courthouse in Ware County was built about 1825 in Waresborough, the original county seat. It was a large, one-story log building with two small side rooms for offices. It is said that the jury often retired to the woods to contemplate their verdict until a larger structure was built at Waresborough. In 1873 the county seat was moved to Waycross where a small, wooden courthouse was built. Unfortunately, it burned soon thereafter. The old courthouse at Waresborough was still standing, and, while the city fathers slept, it was moved and rebuilt at Waycross. A prominent citizen of Waycross is said to have paid for the rebuilding. A three-story brick courthouse was built in 1891 at a cost of $3,100. This served the county until 1957 when a modern structure was erected entirely of Georgia marble.

The county is named for Nicholas Ware of Augusta, a member of the Georgia House and U. S. Senate. The county seat, formerly known as Tebeauville, derived the name of Waycross from its function as a crossway of several railroads.

Augusta   *RICHMOND*   *1959*

One of eight original counties, Richmond County, designated the Colonial Parish of St. Paul in 1758, was changed to Richmond by the Constitution of 1777. It is named for the Duke of Richmond, a friend of the colonies in Parliament, while the county seat honors the mother of King George III.

Court sessions were at Brownsboro until the first courthouse was built in 1784. In 1790 a second courthouse was established in an old home on Bay Street in Augusta. The Government House built on Telfair Street in 1801 then served as the courthouse. Another courthouse, a three-story building adorned with a cupola and clock tower, was built in 1820 on Greene Street at a cost of $100,000. Wings were added in 1870, and it was remodeled again in 1892.

Completed in 1959 at a cost of $2,800,000 by the Beer Construction Company, the present courthouse stands on the same site. This building, designed by Scroggs, Ewing, Kukle & Wade, reflects the style and architecture of an urban municipal complex. A monument to Georgia's three signers of the Declaration of Independence, Button Gwinnett, George Walton, and Lyman Hall, faces the building.

Americus　　　　　*SUMTER*　　　　　*1959*

The first Sumter County courthouse was built in 1834, soon after the creation of the county in 1831. A second courthouse was built in 1848, serving until the third courthouse, a handsome two-story brick structure was built in 1887. The fourth and present courthouse, a modern design by E. Oren Smith, was completed in 1959 for $740,000 by the Barber Construction Company. The bell in the yard was part of the 1887 courthouse.

The county was carved from Lee County, honoring General Thomas Sumter of South Carolina. The origin of the name Americus, the county seat, is uncertain but apparently it was not named in honor of Amerigo Vespucci, the Italian navigator. A visitor in 1914 reported that "the streets are paved with wood blocks and there are forty miles of paved sidewalks."

At Souther Field near Americus, Charles A. Lindberg made his first solo flight.

173

Calhoun   *GORDON*   *1961*

This beautiful brick and white marble courthouse was erected in 1961 by the Gann Construction Company for $400,000 from designs by Cunningham & Forehand. The first courthouse, a two-story brick building enclosed by a picket fence, was built in 1852 soon after the county was organized in 1850. All of the records were removed from the building during the War Between the States and are preserved. In 1888, the original records were again saved when the courthouse was demolished by a severe storm. A second courthouse was completed in 1889 for $14,000 and served until completion of the present building.

The county is named for William Washington Gordon of Savannah, the first president of the Central of Georgia Railroad and the first Georgian to graduate from West Point Military Academy. An election was held to determine the location of the county seat; "Railroad" won over "Center." It was later renamed Calhoun for the distinguished Senator John C. Calhoun of South Carolina, an exponent of the theory that any state could nullify any act of Congress with which it disagreed. The town was rebuilt after General Sherman had ordered the town destroyed during the War Between the States.

New Echota, near Calhoun, served as the capital of the Cherokee nation, where Sequoyah invented the Cherokee alphabet.

Dalton   *WHITFIELD*   *1961*

The first courthouse in Whitfield County, a frame structure was burned by the Union army in October 1864. The second courthouse, completed in 1891, was a two-story brick building with a clock steeple and tower. It was later torn down to make way for the present building. A design of Abreu & Robeson, it was completed in 1961 for one million dollars by the T. L. Kiker Construction Company.

Whitfield, created from Murray County in 1851, is named for Reverend George Whitefield of Savannah; the spelling was changed to reflect the proper pronunciation. The county seat of Dalton, originally Cross Plains, was changed to honor a civil engineer of the area.

Dublin   *LAURENS*   *1962*

Laurens County's fifth courthouse, with traditional facade but no clock tower, was designed by Cunningham & Forehand and built for $900,000 by Aaron Torch & Sons in 1962.

Sumpterville was the first county seat, where the first sessions of court met in 1808 near the home of Peter Thomas. Peter Early, later governor, was the presiding judge, with John Clark, son of Revolutionary War General Elijah Clarke, the solicitor-general. A temporary courthouse was built for $36 in 1811. The county seat was moved to Dublin where a second, two-story courthouse was built with the courtroom on the first floor, rather than the traditional second floor. It was later moved to another location and used as a boarding house, wagon shop, and hospital. The next courthouse, completed in 1895, served until the present structure was completed.

Laurens, one of Georgia's largest counties, was created in 1807 and named for Colonel John Laurens of South Carolina; the county seat was named for the capital of Ireland.

Franklin   *HEARD*   *1964*

The first courthouse in Heard County burned in 1893, and the second, erected in 1894, served until the new courthouse was built in 1964. It has been described as "looking more like a depot," with the modern structure of brick veneer and concrete block not in the rural county tradition.

Heard County is named for famed Tory fighter Governor Stephen Heard, while the county seat derives its name from the great Benjamin Franklin.

Many Indian mounds are located in Heard County, including the mythical "Lovers' Leap" where two Indian lovers, seeking peace for their tribes, jumped to their deaths from a stone cliff.

The county was constituted in 1830 from parts of Carroll, Coweta and Troup counties.

Sylvania   *SCREVEN*   *1964*

Screven County, named for General James Screven, has had eight courthouses, or places of holding court, since 1793. The first was the home of Benjamin Lanier; the second, Benjamin Warren's house near Beaverdam Creek; the third, a small courthouse built in "The Town of Jacksonborough"; and the fourth was a facility completed in 1832 for $3200. It was "painted and ceiled and lined with inch plank, properly seasoned . . . ."

The county seat was moved to Sylvania in 1848 and a new courthouse was built, using some material from the old one. It is reported that Sherman burned this courthouse in 1864, necessitating the sixth courthouse, which was completed in 1869 by David Parker for $3500. The seventh courthouse, a distinctive brick building with an ornate clock tower, was built for $15,000. It was described as the "Most notable building Screven County has ever had."

The present courthouse, located out of the business district, is a one-story brick building designed by Sewell & Associates, providing efficient quarters for the courts and county offices. It was built by McKnight Construction Company for $500,000.

Lyons   *TOOMBS*   *1964*

The first courthouse in Toombs County was completed in 1906, a year after it was created from Emanuel, Montgomery, and Tattnall counties. The brick structure served until it was destroyed by fire in 1917.

The present courthouse, completed in 1964, was designed by Alexander Blair. Total construction cost of this modern brick and sandstone structure was $46,113.

The county is named for the fiery Georgian, Robert Toombs, Confederate General and Secretary of State in the Jefferson Davis Cabinet. Inscribed on his tombstone, at his request, is the phrase: "Here lies an unpardoned Rebel." The county seat, Lyons, was founded as a depot on the Macon & Savannah Railroad.

The county is the "Onion (Vidalia, that is) Capital of the World."

Hiawassee   *TOWNS*   *1964*

Towns County, which honors Governor George W. Towns of Talbot County, was constituted in 1856 shortly after his death.

The first courthouse was built on the public square in 1857. A second courthouse, completed in 1905, served until the present building was erected in 1964. A two-story, flat-roofed brick veneer building, it is distinguished by its arches and columns.

Hiawassee, the county seat, derives its name from the Cherokee word for "meadow." Brasstown Bald, the state's highest peak at 4,784 feet, is the county's most popular tourist attraction. According to legend, a flood destroyed everything and everyone, except a few Cherokee families who landed on top of the mountain in a canoe. The "Great Spirit" killed all the trees on top of the mountain, so the survivors could plant crops until the flood waters subsided.

Cleveland   *WHITE*   *1964*

White County's first courthouse was built in 1860. This building served as the courthouse for over one hundred years, when it was replaced in 1964 by the present courthouse and converted to a museum.

White County was founded in 1857 from a portion of Habersham County, after numerous attempts to create it had failed. It is named in honor of Newton County's David White for his invaluable role in the creation of White County. The county seat, originally known as Mount Yonah, was named for Revolutionary hero Colonel Ben Cleveland.

Georgia's Alpine village, Helen, is a major tourist attraction in White County, as is Unicoi State Park and nearby Anna Ruby Falls.

Clarkesville   *HABERSHAM*   *1965*

Though Habersham County was created in 1818 from the Cherokee cessions of 1817, the first record of a courthouse indicates one which was built in 1832, only to be blown up in 1898. The second courthouse, built in 1898, served until the present courthouse was built in 1965. It is a modern building of faced brick on concrete block.

Cornelia, the largest town, is the location of the "Big Red Apple," a monument to the apple industry.

The county was named for Revolutionary War hero Major Joseph Habersham, who later served in Congress and as postmaster-general during the Washington, Adams, and Jefferson administrations. The county seat honors Governor John Clark.

Dahlonega   *LUMPKIN*   *1965*

Lumpkin County is named for Wilson Lumpkin, congressman, senator, and governor, who was commissioned by President Monroe to mark the boundary between Georgia and Florida.

The present courthouse is a radical departure from its predecessor, one of the most historic buildings in Georgia. The older building was completed in 1836 for $6,850. The contractor was paid in gold bullion. It served until 1965 when it was converted into the Gold Museum.

The first county seat of Lumpkin was the gold rush boom town of Auraria, known as Nuckollsville when the county seat was moved to Dahlonega in 1833. A log cabin courthouse was erected there on the present Town Square. Dahlonega is the Cherokee word for "yellow metal." With the discovery of gold in California in 1849, the director of the U. S. Mint, which had been established in Dahlonega, tried to stop the exodus with the well-known "There's gold in them thar hills, boys." Visitors may still try their hand at panning gold in the "mines," designed as an exciting tourist attraction.

Marietta *COBB* *1966*

The first courthouse in Cobb County, a one-story, one-room log building, was built in 1834. Used for all the courts and for Sunday church services, it became the pride of the frontier Marietta. In 1838 a square, hip-roofed, two-story white frame courthouse, 60 x 80 feet, was erected in the center of town. Another courthouse, built in 1852, was destroyed in 1864 by a fire probably set by federal soldiers. The fourth courthouse was completed in 1873 and served the county until the modern courthouse and office building was completed in 1966.

Cobb County was formed from Cherokee County in 1832 and is named for Thomas Willis Cobb, Congressman, U. S. Senator, and trustee of the University of Georgia. The county seat is named for Cobb's wife.

Decatur   *DeKALB*   *1967*

DeKalb County, created in 1822, is named for Baron Johann De Kalb, German Revolutionary War officer who was wounded in South Carolina and died in a British prison. The county seat is named in honor of Commodore Stephen Decatur.

A small frame courthouse was erected a year after the creation of DeKalb from Fayette, Gwinnett, and Henry counties. A second wooden building was destroyed by fire in 1842; the third courthouse met the same fate in 1898. Constructed in 1916, the fourth courthouse is the home of the DeKalb Historical Society. The modern courthouse which was completed in 1967 reflects the tremendous growth of the area.

DOUGHERTY

The Dougherty County Courthouse provides the city of Albany with administrative headquarters with joint maintenance by the county and city.

Created in 1853 from Baker, the county is named for Charles Dougherty, an attorney and advocate of state's rights. The county seat, founded by Colonel Nelson Tift, is reportedly named for the capital of New York. When the county was created, one of the first acts was to call for bids on land for public buildings. Court was held in rented rooms above the Post Office while bids were taken for a courthouse and jail. The buildings were completed by slaves, for whom the county paid thirty-five dollars per month. The first courthouse and jail, completed in 1856, was a two-story building constructed of handmade brick with a cupola. This courthouse served until 1904, when it was replaced. Fire struck in 1966 and destroyed a substantial portion of the structure. At the time of the fire, the building had been scheduled for demolition and most of the offices had been vacated. The present courthouse, in the planning stage at the time of the fire, was occupied October 1, 1968.

Clayton   *RABUN*   *1968*

The county, created in 1818 from Cherokee Cessions, is named for one of Georgia's governors, William Rabun. The county seat honors Judge Augustin S. Clayton. The famous Tallulah Gorge is one of the better known attractions in the county.

A log structure built in 1824 was the first courthouse to serve this north Georgia county. The second courthouse, built in 1836, was in use until 1908 when the third courthouse was erected. By 1966, two more courthouses had been outgrown. The present building, next to the old one, was built by Hagman Construction Company from designs by John H. Hoite & Associates. Financed by a $500,000 bond issue, its attractive and functional design is a good example of modern courthouses.

Hartwell **HART** *1971*

The first courthouse, a two-story frame structure, was completed in 1854, the year after Hart County was organized from Elbert and Franklin counties. This courthouse served until a second courthouse was built in 1856. It was destroyed by fire in 1900. A third courthouse, completed in 1902, was destroyed by fire in 1967.

The present Hart County Courthouse, built in 1971, has masonry bearing walls with steel floor framing and is typical of the postwar courthouse architecture.

The county and county seat honor Revolutionary heroine Nancy Hart. Hart County has the distinction of being the only county in Georgia named for a woman. It is the site of Hartwell Dam on the Savannah River.

Buchanan   *HARALSON*   *1972*

The county is named for General Hugh A. Haralson and the county seat for James Buchanan, the last Democratic president before the War Between the States. The location of the county seat was decided by the judges of the Inferior Court and was incorporated several years after the county was created in 1856.

In 1972, a modern steel-framed brick veneer courthouse was built about a mile from Buchanan, setting a trend toward moving courthouses from "The Square." The previous courthouse, built in 1891, still stands on the town square, where it serves as a museum and community activities building. Little is known of an earlier courthouse built shortly after the county was organized.

Columbus　　　　　*MUSCOGEE*　　　　　*1972*

Muscogee County's gleaming steel and glass Municipal County Building is a far cry from courthouses of earlier eras, but typical of urban areas requiring enormous space to serve the growing needs of the county. This building was completed in 1972 by Jordan-Groves Construction Company from plans by Biggers, Scarborough, Neal, Crisp & Clark. It was financed by $11.4 million dollar Building Authority certificates. In 1970 Muscogee County and the City of Columbus merged, thus forming the first consolidated government in Georgia.

The first courthouse was a rough wood structure built soon after the county was created in 1826. In 1838 a brick structure with Doric columns supporting the portico was erected. In 1896, this courthouse was replaced by a larger one, which served until razed in 1969 to make way for the present building. At a total cost of $11,400,000, it is, at this time, the most expensive courthouse building in Georgia.

The county is named for the Muscogee Indians, the county seat in honor of Christopher Columbus.

Lakeland   *LANIER*   *1973*

Lanier is one of the youngest counties in Georgia, and has one of the most modern courthouses in the state. It was built in 1973 of brick veneer with steel framing and floor system by Lewis Brothers Company for $430,000 from plans by Thomson Sanders. It replaced the first courthouse which was completed in 1921, a year after the county was created.

Lanier County is named in honor of Georgia poet Sidney Lanier. The name Lakeland is derived from the many natural lakes that dot the area. The ten-mile, Lakeland-owned railroad, connecting Lakeland and Naylor, was said to be the only railroad in the nation owned by a municipality. It was abandoned for lack of business.

Gainesville   *HALL*   *1975*

The first courthouse in Hall was a simple wooden structure built in 1833. It was replaced by a brick building which was destroyed in 1936 by the worst tornado in Georgia's history, which left 170 people dead and nearly a thousand injured. The present courthouse, constructed in 1937 for $153,700, is a modern structure although it retains the traditional clock tower of earlier times. A substantial addition was made in 1975 to accomodate the growing needs of the county.

Created in 1818 from Cherokee lands, Hall County is named for Dr. Lyman Hall, one of Georgia's signers of the Declaration of Independence. Some sources indicate that the county seat is named for the Gaines family, early settlers, while other sources say it is named for General Edmund Gaines, for whom the county seat of Clay County is named.

Rome   *FLOYD*   *1976*

Floyd County was created from Cherokee County in 1832. The first courthouse was a log cabin built in 1833 at Livingston. A temporary structure, built when Rome became the county seat, served until a third courthouse was completed in 1893. It was designed by architects Bruce & Morgan and built by Patton Sash, Door and Construction Company for $49,925. Its walls were five bricks thick, with the original design calling for clocks in the tower, but none were ever installed. The building was remodeled in 1938 at a cost of $72,000.

The present courthouse, previously the Post Office and U. S. Court House, was acquired from the federal government in 1976 and renovated by the Abco Builders, Inc. for $2,229,500 from plans by Bothwell, Jenkins & Slay, architects.

The county is named for General John Floyd, hero of the War of 1812 and congressman. The first county seat was Livingston but in 1838 it was changed to Rome, which spans seven hills, as does the Italian city for which it is named.

Cumming   *FORSYTH*   *1977*

Forsyth, created from Cherokee County in 1832, is named for John Forsyth, distinguished Georgian who negotiated the sale of Florida from Spain to the United States. The county seat is named for Augusta's William Cumming, a hero of the War of 1812.

The first courthouse was built in Forsyth County in 1832, serving the county until 1900 when it was destroyed by fire. The second courthouse, built in 1905, was destroyed by fire in 1973. For several years the county used temporary buildings as the courthouse until the present courthouse, a beautiful brick structure was completed and occupied in 1977.

Colquitt   *MILLER*   *1977*

Miller County has had four courthouses. The current one, costing $919,660, was dedicated on July 2, 1977. It is a modern brick design with four arches instead of the traditional columns flanking the entrance. Its predecessor, a two-story brick building with a traditional clock tower, built in 1906 for $20,227, was totally destroyed by fire in 1974. Two earlier courthouses served the county from its creation in 1856 until 1906.

Miller is named for Andrew J. Miller of Augusta, distinguished jurist and legislator, recognized as an early champion of the legal rights of women. Colquitt, the county seat, is named for Walter T. Colquitt, judge, U. S. Senator, and father of Governor Alfred Colquitt.

Savannah   *CHATHAM*   *1978*

When John and Charles Wesley arrived in the Colony in February 1736, it is said that John began his ministry with a sermon delivered to a noisy crowd in the new courthouse which also served as the church. This was the first courthouse in Georgia. The next courthouse was a large brick structure built in 1765. A third was built in 1833, serving until 1889 when the fourth building was completed. This structure still stands. The present courthouse was completed in 1978. While efficient and utilitarian, it varies from the traditional Savannah architecture.

Chatham was created by the Constitution of 1777 from St. Philip and Christ Church parishes, and is named for the Earl of Chatham, William Lord Pitt, one of England's most prominent prime ministers. Savannah is one of the most historic cities in the United States. It was laid out in 1733 by Oglethorpe and probably derived its name from the Spanish word "Sabanna," meaning grassy plain.

Dawsonville **DAWSON** *1978*

This beautiful courthouse, one of Georgia's newest, was completed and dedicated in 1978. Modern in design, it is a two-story brick structure with parking area. The spacious courtroom seats 175 people and along the building's easy access corridors are located the various county offices. The total cost was $799,781, which was financed by a federal grant. The architect for the building was Bailey Allegret, and the builder was the Ledbetter Brothers Company.

The original courthouse was built in 1858 soon after the county was created. A two-story brick structure with a gabled roof, it is reminiscent of many early Georgia courthouses built with simple lines without facade or clock tower.

Dawson County was created in 1857 from parts of Gilmer and Lumpkin counties. The county and county seat honor U. S. Judge William C. Dawson, a hero of the War of 1812, who served in the U. S. House and Senate.

Blairsville   **UNION**   *1978*

Residents of Union County were strong supporters of the federal government. When the question of names came up in the Legislature, John Thomas, the area representative, suggested "Union, for none but Union men reside in it." The county seat Blairsville, laid out in 1838, was named for Kentuckian Francis P. Blair, who presided over the first Republican Convention in 1856.

The first courthouse in Union County was built in 1833 soon after the county's creation in 1832 from the Cherokee Cession. It served until 1859 when it suffered the fate of many courthouse — FIRE. A two-story brick courthouse was built on the same site in 1860. After 110 years, in 1970, the building was found unsafe for use as a public building. In 1974 a modern one-story brick building housing county offices was built. The courtroom was completed in 1978.

Cusseta   *CHATTAHOOCHEE*   *1979*

Chattahoochee County was formed from parts of Marion and Muscogee counties in 1854, and named for the river which forms its western boundary. A vast portion of Fort Benning, home of the Infantry, is in the county. The county seat, known as Sand Town, was at one time the site of the village where Oglethorpe made a treaty with the Lower Creek Indians in 1739.

The first courthouse was built in Cusseta, designated the county seat in 1854. This structure was a large square, two-story building of select heart pine cut and erected by slave labor. It was the oldest frame courthouse in Georgia until it was moved to Westville in 1974 and restored under the sponsorship of the State Bar of Georgia.

When the present courthouse was completed in 1979, one county official is reported to have said that the commissioners "will replace a priceless jewel of an antique courthouse with a cracker box, because that's all the money they've got."

Originals

Georgia Courthouses on the National Registry

Courthouses, still intact, used for other purposes

DeKalb	Government House (Richmond)
Lumpkin	Bartow
White	Floyd
Haralson	Marion
Chattahoochee	Union
Campbell	Dawson

Courthouses, still in use, prior to 1980

Thomas	Morgan
Baldwin	Randolph
Meriwether	Oglethorpe
Hall	Berrien
Hancock	

Courthouses, listed under thematic nomination

Appling	Elbert	Montgomery
Atkinson	Evans	Murray
Bacon	Fayette	Newton
Baker	Floyd	Paulding
Banks	Franklin	Peach
Barrow	Fulton	Pierce
Bartow	Gilmer	Pike
Ben Hill	Glascock	Pulaski
Bleckley	Greene	Schley
Brooks	Gwinnett	Seminole
Bulloch	Harris	Stephens
Burke	Henry	Stewart
Butts	Irwin	Talbot
Camden	Jackson	Taliaferro
Candler	Jasper	Terrell
Carroll	Jeff Davis	Tift
Charlton	Jefferson	Treutlen
Chatooga	Jenkins	Turner
Clay	Johnson	Twiggs
Clinch	Jones	Upson
Colquitt	Lamar	Walker
Columbia	Lee	Walton
Coweta	Liberty	Warren
Crawford	Lincoln	Washington
Dade	Long	Wayne
Decatur	Lowndes	Webster
Dodge	Macon	Wheeler
Dooly	Madison	Wilcox
Early	Marion	Wilkes
Effingham	Monroe	Worth

When the Fayette Courthouse was renovated in the 1960s, the main beam was removed intact and converted to a bench. The 58-foot timber is believed to be the longest hand-hewn in America.

The tiny chapel which adjoins the courtroom of the Pulaski County Courthouse has been the scene of many weddings and, according to local legend, a place of solitude for attorneys faced with difficult cases.

The Floyd County Courthouse, built in 1892 by the famed architectural firm of Bruce & Morgan, is decorated with a row of gargoyles for a string course. As far as is known, these are the only gargoyles in Georgia — at least on courthouses.

The Oglethorpe County Courthouse, built of a variety of native materials, is one of the most picturesque in the state. The balcony was used primarily as the platform where laws, rules and announcements were "proclaimed" which led to the use of a "platform" by aspiring political candidates who made the most of the balcony to address the voters.

The stained glass window, featuring the Great Seal of Georgia, in the Chattooga County Courthouse has brought more fame to the courtroom than some of the typically "sensational" trials which bring temporary attention — or notoriety to the county.

The jury box has been completely renovated and restored in the "old" Haralson County Courthouse which is being converted to civic and cultural activities in the area.

The Seth Thomas clock became a part of the tower on the Hancock County Courthouse a century ago. Although it has been electrified recently, it has been in continuous use under the tender loving care of successive dedicated "Clock Custodians". When the clock strikes twelve everyone in Sparta knows it's time for lunch.

1. Tradition has it that Confederate soldiers, with rifles at shoulder arms, face North. On the lawn of the modern Douglas County Courthouse, this veteran stands at ease. 2. In many cases, the Confederate monument predates the courthouse. In Stewart County, this "sentry" was the silent witness to the fire which destroyed an older courthouse. 3. Wreathed in spring blossoms, the Confederate monument on the lawn of the Taylor County Courthouse is very much a part of the heritage of Georgia. Although not always on the courthouse square, there is a Confederate monument somewhere in every county seat.

The only Confederate to be a victim of an automobile accident is the old general who stood at the intersection of the main streets in Hawkinsville. After being struck by a car, he was moved to a safer place on the lawn of the Pulaski County Courthouse where his "broken hand" had been a tourist attraction — until parties unknown had decided on some plaster of paris surgery — to the dismay of many county residents.

The memorial to Crawford Long, the Georgia doctor who was the first to use ether in surgery, is a prominent feature of the Madison County Courthouse square in Danielsville, the birthplace of Dr. Long.

The Pulaski County Courthouse was built more than a century ago when its spacious courtroom was one of the largest in the state.

Old Government House, Augusta

Photograph by James R. Lockhart for
Dept. of Natural Resources, Historic Preservation Section

United States
Court Houses
in Georgia

United States Court House, Albany

United States Court House, Brunswick

United States Court House, Atlanta

United States Court House, Augusta

United States Court House, Athens

United States Court House, Columbus

United States Court House, Gainesville

United States Court House, Macon

United States Court House, Newnan

United States Court House, Rome

United States Court House, Savannah

United States Court House,
Valdosta

United States Court House,
Waycross

BIBLIOGRAPHY

Knight, Lucian Lamar, *Georgia's Landmarks, Memorials and Legends, Vol. I and II,* Byrd Printing Company, Atlanta, 1913-14

Reminiscences of Famous Georgians, Vol. I and II, Franklin Turner Company, Atlanta, 1907-08

Moore, Charles, *Know Your County,* reprinted from The Atlanta Constitution

White, *Statistics of the State of Georgia,* 1849 Edition

Various published County Histories and Georgia Historical Commission Markers

Judicial Facilities Inventory, Space Management Consultants, Inc., Atlanta, 1976

United States 1980 Census of Population and Housing, U. S. Department of Commerce, March 1981

Georgia Official Directory of U. S. Congressmen, State and County Officers, Secretary of State, January 1983

Foundations of Government, 1976, Association of County Commissioners of Georgia

Georgia Official and Statistical Register, 1977-78

The 1982 Georgia County Guide, Coop Extension Service, Tifton

Georgia Official and Statistical Register, 1979-80

Griffin, Louis and John E. Talmadge, *Georgia Journalism,* 1763-1950

Georgia Historical Quarterlies

Johnson, Amanda, *Georgia as Colony and State*

Knight, Lucian Lamar, *Standard History of Georgia and Georgians*

Saye, Albert B., *Constitutional History of Georgia*

Candler, Allen D., Editor, *Colonial Records of the State of Georgia*

Lanning, John T., *Diplomatic History of Georgia*

Vanstory, Burnette, *Georgia's Land of the Golden Isles*

Coleman, Kenneth, *The American Revolution in Georgia*

Candler, Allen, D., Editor, *Revolutionary Records of the State of Georgia*

Candler, Allen D., Editor, *Confederate Records of the State of Georgia*

Arnett, Alex M., *Populist Movement in Georgia*

Thompson, Clara Mildred, *Reconstruction in Georgia*

Cosnell, C. B. and C. D. Anderson, *Government and Administration of Georgia*

Hughes, M. Clyde, *County Government in Georgia*

Cook, James F., *Governors of Georgia*

Mellichamp, Josephine, *Senators of Georgia*

Linley, John, *Guide to the Architecture of Georgia*

Hammond, Bray, *Banks and Politics in American from the Revolutionary to the Civil War*

Reese, T. R., *Colonial Georgia*

Adler, J. R., *The First South*

Cohn, David L., *The Life and Times of King Cotton*

Henderson, James, CBE, *The Frigates*

Weinstein, Leo, *17th Century European Culture*

Henderson, M. B., *18th Century History of Europe*

Probet, Denis and Furet, *The French Revolution*

Bruin, Goeffrey, *Rise of Modern Europe*

Biographical Directory of The American Congress, 1774-1971

Surveys — Superior Court Clerks; Probate Judges, 1977-81

Coleman, Kenneth, *A History of Georgia*

Linton, Calvin D., *The Bicentennial Almanac*

INDEX